To T[...]

Happy [...]

With love from

Viv & Dave xx

LEGENDS OF THE WILD WEST

ROBERT EDELSTEIN

CENTENNIAL BOOKS

LEGENDS
OF THE WILD
WEST

ROBERT EDELSTEIN

CENTENNIAL BOOKS

46

168

96

60

CONTENTS

LEGENDS OF THE WILD WEST

A GLANCE BACK AT A NOTORIOUS PLACE AND TIME THAT STILL FEEDS THE POWERFUL AMERICAN DREAM.

THEY CAME IN A CLOUD OF DUST, heading from somewhere safe to a place beyond borders. They were determined homesteaders grasping posters that promised them acres to till if they'd only "Go West, Young Man." They were hungry prospectors itching to get their feet wet in streams gleaming with specks of gold. They were ranchers and railroaders looking to expand both their pocketbooks and the pathways to the Pacific. They were mountain men telling tall tales, and riders and shooters feeding a fantasy of guns and glory they'd seen in Buffalo Bill's shows. And they were newly paid cowboys heading to the boomtown saloon looking to get loaded, followed by peace officers keeping their pistols that way, just in case trouble came along with them.

This much we know: The frontier of the American West from the end of the Civil War to the start of the next century was an untamed place. It was filled with Native peoples working their own land and then striving to keep it against all odds; bitter feelings left over from the years of North-South battles; and powers from Europe and Mexico ready to fight for their territorial claims.

And what exactly did all of this produce? The most potent and notorious cocktail the U.S. ever shook into being: the Wild West. Take one shot of oversize dreams, one shot of determined disappointment, one shot of homemade saloon liquor and add one shot from the barrel of a Henry rifle. Mix like crazy, and then watch out.

More than a century after its most famous names lived big (and decades since the days when Hollywood

and hearsay helped to carve those names even more deeply into the American consciousness), the Wild West still stands as a time and place where the seemingly endless spaces were seen as one great challenge. The aim was to explore, to win, to expand and to plant your flag in as dramatic and significant a way as possible. Even today, the ghosts of that era still inspire people to dream big and press forward, come hell or high water.

"It's really astonishing that such a short period in which, in the broader trend of history, so few things happened, has become this iconic representation of the American past," says Richard White, PhD, a professor emeritus of American history at Stanford University. "I think the answer is largely due to this idea of

You'll find stories of people striving to make their mark their own way—and to keep those stories from being spun out of control—in these pages that celebrate the notorious days of the Wild West. There are tales told from lawmen and the lawless they tracked, of the most famous shots fired and the top guns that were brought along for all the action, legendary ladies, dynamic duos, fast-drawing figures, motion picture heroes, the West's frontier president, its most iconic and misunderstood figure and its one true genius. They're the names that turned the real West into the mythic one that lives on. Or, as Patty Limerick, PhD, a professor of American Western history at the University of Colorado Boulder puts it, "It's that phrase, 'the Wild West'—it's got an immortality about it." ★

William "Buffalo Bill" Cody helped spread the lore of the Wild West throughout the nation.

CHAPTER ONE

HOW THE WEST GOT WILD

TIME LINE OF THE OLD WEST

THE FIERY FEW DECADES THAT CHANGED THE PLAINS FOREVER.

PASSAGE OF THE KANSAS-NEBRASKA ACT

The bill, which created the territories of Kansas and Nebraska, left the decision of bringing slavery west to its residents. Northerners and Southerners poured into the territories to affect change, often by violence, leading to what became known as Bleeding Kansas, and setting the template for Civil War.

START OF THE CIVIL WAR

The election of Abraham Lincoln, running on a platform to end slavery, led, on February 4, 1861, to secession and the birth of the Confederate States of America. A little more than two months later, Confederate forces fired on Fort Sumter in South Carolina, beginning four years of bloody conflict.

THE CIVIL WAR ENDS

Less than a month after the assassination of President Lincoln and after a monthlong period of **surrenders by Confederate generals**, President Andrew Johnson declared an end to armed resistance. One day later, Confederate President Jefferson Davis was captured.

"WILD BILL" RUNS IN *HARPER'S*

The magazine story covered the exploits of Wild Bill Hickok, elevating the gambler turned lawman into a legend. The publication of the widely inaccurate, wildly popular article is now regarded as the official start of the Wild West.

| MAY 30, 1854 | FEBRUARY 19, 1861 | APRIL 12, 1861 | MAY 20, 1862 | MAY 9, 1865 | FEBRUARY 13, 1866 | FEBRUARY 1867 |

THE BASCOM AFFAIR

The brother of Chiricahua Apache chief Cochise was killed by troops led by Lt. **George Bascom** after he falsely accused Cochise of a kidnapping. The killing came after a standoff between Bascom and Cochise that led to deaths on both sides and inspired the Apache Wars.

LINCOLN SIGNS THE HOMESTEAD ACT INTO LAW

The act made millions of acres of land in the West available for qualified adults (meaning those who had never attacked the U.S. government). The law, which had been controversial prior to the Civil War, eventually led to the settlement of 270 million acres over four years by 16 million homesteaders, including freed slaves.

ROBBING BANKS...IN BROAD DAYLIGHT

Liberty, Missouri's Clay County Savings Association, owned by Northern-favoring Republicans, was robbed of the modern-day equivalent of more than $1 million. A bystander was killed as about 10 riders came into town, with two entering the bank. Long considered to be among the likely culprits: brothers **Jesse and Frank James.**

DODGE CITY FOUNDED

The territory 5 miles west of Fort Dodge had become a pivot point for the railroad, cattle drives and the buffalo trade. Once fully established as **Dodge City**, it quickly outdid Abilene, Kansas, as the most notorious stop in the West, where Bat Masterson and Wyatt Earp plied their gun-toting trades.

MURDER AND MAYHEM, AS GUNS RULE THE WEST

Notorious outlaw **Billy the Kid** was killed by Sheriff Pat Garrett on July 14, 1881. Three months later, on October 26, the Earp brothers and Doc Holliday met the Clanton Gang in the Gunfight at the O.K. Corral. And on April 3, 1882, Jesse James' fate was sealed at the hands of Robert Ford—and a bullet to the back of the head.

U.S. CENSUS BUREAU DECLARES THE FRONTIER CLOSED

The 11th U.S. Census concluded that, given the movement of the population across the country, it would no longer track westward migration, effectively stating that the frontier had disappeared. On March 3, 1891, President **Benjamin Harrison** signed the Forest Reserve Act, setting aside lands that might once have been available for homesteading or railroads.

THE FRONTIER THESIS

Frederick Jackson Turner read his paper "The Significance of the Frontier in American History" to the American Historical Society in Chicago, putting a name to the myth of the American West. The "Frontier thesis" talked of the importance of American fascination with the frontier and how that changed the country significantly; it's a fascination that continues to this day.

MAY 10, 1869	JUNE 1872	JUNE 25, 1876	1881–1882	SEPTEMBER 4, 1886	JUNE 2, 1890	DECEMBER 29, 1890	JULY 12, 1893

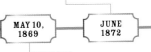

CUSTER'S LAST STAND

Gen. George Armstrong Custer and 250 of his 7th Cavalry forces were killed at the **Battle of Little Bighorn** after the general strategically misjudged the size of Native American forces they had come to kill. The astonishing loss propelled the U.S. government forward in its redoubled commitment to rid the plains of Native tribes.

GERONIMO SURRENDERS, ENDING THE APACHE WARS

The warrior was arrested in Fort Grant, Arizona, surrendering to First Lt. Charles Gatewood, whom Geronimo respected for his perseverance in the pursuit. Twenty-three years later, on his deathbed, a regretful Geronimo reportedly told his nephew, "I should have fought until I was the last man alive."

WOUNDED KNEE MASSACRE

Two weeks after the killing of Sioux Chief **Sitting Bull**, a mass shooting of captured Lakotas by U.S. Army forces led to the deaths of at least 150 Lakota men, women and children. The massacre meant the end of Indian-U.S. conflicts and the continuation of a legend that inspired Native peoples to seek a return to their way of life.

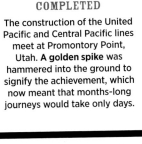

FIRST TRANSCONTINENTAL RAILROAD IS COMPLETED

The construction of the United Pacific and Central Pacific lines meet at Promontory Point, Utah. **A golden spike** was hammered into the ground to signify the achievement, which now meant that months-long journeys would take only days.

The West, with its wide-open spaces and opportunities, became an unknowable but unstoppable lure for men seeking a new life.

CALL WILD
OF THE

**THE UNITED STATES EXPANDED THROUGH
THE PLAINS AFTER THE CIVIL WAR, BUT NO ONE
EXPECTED THOSE DAYS WOULD BE SO
OUT OF CONTROL. HERE'S WHY IT HAPPENED.**

AT FIRST, THEY ALL FOUGHT for it—the British, the French, the Spanish, the Mexicans and more. But then, after centuries of battles, the Americans, who had settled in the East, declared their independence and were, in time, able to turn their eyes and hearts toward the far coast. It was the wide-open American West, with its plains and possibilities, its land and a legacy just waiting to be built. It was all there. But what made those days out West so...*wild*?

"To many Americans, the Wild West represents freedom, symbolically and literally, and that idea has enormous power," says Durwood Ball, an associate professor at the University of New Mexico. And the tale of the pathway to gain that power—and the myths it all built—became incredibly complicated.

In the 1850s, the vast territory beyond the Mississippi remained, with notable exceptions, the great unknown—and its lure was unmistakable, its exploration as inevitable as the cry "Go West, Young Man," that many folks erroneously believe came from Horace Greeley. The author of the quote is a mystery, but its message is anything but: What better travel incentive could one get—especially for those young men?

The American West was all set up for an enormous, high-caliber struggle through decades of expansion. And here are the five things that made those adrenaline-filled days so memorable.

Coveting the Land

It would be hard to find so many acres with such hearty stretches of natural resources. The land was rich, not only for frontier farmers but for trappers and then miners and, later, businessmen trying their hand at bringing gold up from the ground. "It was stocked with extraordinarily rich untapped resources, and it was about getting your people on the ground and in that space to

> ## "Armed violence and brutality in Kansas was the spark that created both the Civil War and the Wild West."
>
> *Professor Emeritus Richard White*

---

convert them," says Ball, about everybody from beaver and fur trappers to the international cattle companies that found profit in the new beef industry. Even the grass itself mattered. "That's the big one, out there on the Great Plains," Ball adds. "The question was how to convert that into commodities, for grazing sheep and cattle on it." Capitalism led to competition in every corner of the map. Few were able to gain the same wealth as famed industrialist John Jacob Astor, who made millions in the fur trade; but everyone who could, tried.

The Bloody Tale of Kansas
No single issue, it seems, led more directly to bloodshed and battles than the Kansas-Nebraska Act of 1854. The question of whether those two territories, smack in the middle of the country, would allow slavery, plus the illegal votes cast on both sides of the issue on the path to statehood, created deadly confrontations. In one infamous skirmish involving the pro-slavery Quantrill's Raiders and the anti-slavery Jayhawkers, William Quantrill and his men killed more than 180 civilians in Lawrence, Kansas, in retaliation for an earlier offense. Once the war ended and the truth settled in that the Northern government had set laws in motion for populating the West without slavery, the Confederate-favored "bushwhackers" continued to fight, and kill, for their political beliefs, with famed figures such as Wild Bill Hickok and Jesse James taking their guns to Kansas towns and then beyond, forging infamous careers. "It was armed violence and brutality and gun fighting," says Richard White, a Stanford University professor emeritus of history. "Kansas is really the spark that sets off the Civil War, and Kansas is also going to be the spark that creates the Wild West."

IMAGE MAKER
Buffalo Bill was, astonishingly, able to capture the action of the Wild West almost as it was happening.

What Women Wanted

In 1848, at the first women's rights convention in the U.S., an agreement was made on a demand to vote, and Susan B. Anthony was jailed for illegally doing so in 1874. In the years between and afterward, men were reading the tea leaves, and they felt threatened by an encroaching loss of identity. "Easterners decided that the rugged West, the outdoor West, the Wild West was a source of rejuvenation, and they were afraid [the country] was becoming too much like Europe," says University of Washington professor John Findlay. "A lot of the fantasy of the West was a response to the idea that the country was becoming too feminized, that women were having too much power, that manliness was disappearing," he says. The solution, it seemed, was to resurrect

that power, at times in all its manly glory. "Out West," says White, "the code of a man was still in order."

The Man with the Plan

The fantasy may have existed, but it came to astonishing light in Buffalo Bill's Wild West shows, with its performances of plains battles in front of thousands of fans, weaving in the myths created by dime novels and offering a view of the Wild West at essentially the same time that actual events were occurring—to the point of introducing Wild Bill Hickok not long after a much-discussed gunfight. It was William Cody's particular genius to create something that was part Barnum & Bailey Circus, part Las Vegas extravaganza and a show as ambitious as the West itself.

"Those shows celebrated the skills of horse-riding, and then they dramatized the gun battles between native peoples and whites, often with Native actors playing Native roles," says Findlay. "People began mythologizing the West as it was going on. I don't know how [Buffalo Bill] did that."

The Seeds of Destiny

It was all this—the endless rootin'-tootin' publicity, the lure of the land and a new start, the bitterness at how the war had turned out and more—that made heading out West and finding your place feel like something of a right, especially if you believed you were particularly entitled. "Theodore Roosevelt articulated this idea of the frontier and the West as a space where white males could go and fulfill their liberty and economic dreams—their destiny," says Ball. Adds Findlay: "Prior to 1861, the country couldn't agree on a transcontinental railroad." Then came the years of Civil War, followed by this extraordinary expansion, and the terribly bloody chapter of making all this movement while pushing an entire people off their own land. It's what Frederick Jackson Turner, the great historian, wrote of in his "Frontier thesis," which spoke of the optimism and individualism of these new settlers, no matter the cost. "This isn't the mythic West. This is what really happened," says Findlay, noting that the Wild West came to a close when the U.S. government shut down the easy purchase of land in 1893: "Those were the last days of the real West. But it became the mythic West too, and the mythic West never dies." ★

WOMEN'S RIGHTS
Susan B. Anthony (above left) and her fellow suffragettes fought for the vote in a gender struggle that helped create the Wild West.

PICTURE PERFECT
Artist Frederic Remington captured this image of the fur trader (above right), which made the life seem more romantic and mythic than it was.

Men and women were both eligible to apply for land after the Homestead Act was passed, and single women "proved up" at a rate competitive with men.

THE 'PROMISED' LAND

THE GOVERNMENT, BIG BUSINESSES AND HORACE GREELEY LURED ORDINARY FOLK WEST WITH THE DEAL OF A LIFETIME—ONE THAT DIDN'T ALWAYS PAN OUT.

A

MERICA IS THE LAND OF dreams—and in the 19th century, the dreams were as big as the open skies over the Plains. They were also as wide as the lush lands beneath those skies, promising bountiful crops you could grow to sell and feed your family, and a house you could build with your own hands, with smoke from the Dutch oven rising through the chimney at night. The men who toiled at thankless jobs back East and all over Europe could fantasize well enough to see those images clearly in their minds. And if they had trouble visualizing, all they had to do was look around them. Newspapers, novels and notices promised a better life out West. All people had to do was pull up stakes and prepare to put down roots that were meant to grow strong. Oh, if only it always worked out that way.

For the people pushing the idea of migration across the country, and for homesteaders who took the bait and went (in the end, the total would be 1.6 million), the movement to the West was a marketing campaign unlike any other in American history. It tapped hype and promoted hope, tempting a population desiring both change and a chance to start over in a mysterious land of opportunity.

That the settlers succeeded in making lives for themselves much less than half the time is now lost to history. What matters more is the idea that, at each step, someone was going to get paid for helping lure the folks out. This was a business of enormous profit.

Posters made the journey seem inevitable, even necessary. "Indian Land for Sale" one promised, with a photo of a supposedly happily departing Native in the frame,

Ho for Kansas!

Brethren, Friends, & Fellow Citizens:
I feel thankful to inform you that the
REAL ESTATE
AND
Homestead Association,
Will Leave Here the
15th of April, 1878,

In pursuit of Homes in the Southwestern
Lands of America, at Transportation
Rates, cheaper than ever
was known before.
For full information inquire of
Benj. Singleton, better known as old Pap,
NO. 5 NORTH FRONT STREET.
Beware of Speculators and Adventurers, as it is a dangerous thing
to fall in their hands.
Nashville, Tenn., March 18, 1878.

alongside the words, "Get a home of your own. Easy payments." By then, an eager young man's head had been filled with the adventures he'd read about in dime novels. You could sit at your desk and sigh about your humdrum existence, or you could follow the trails to a place where you wouldn't have to answer to any boss but yourself.

For decades, this message echoed across the country and around the world. The gist was simple: Come out West and, as one of America's most famous publishers, Horace Greeley, suggested in the 1850s, "grow with the country." He wasn't the first to say it, but he also gets the credit for coining the phrase "Go West, Young Man."

Sending the Message

By the time Greeley began spreading that call of the wild, Americans had already spent years making their passage. The historic economic downturn in 1837, some 100 years prior to the 20th-century's Great Depression, brought banks to a standstill, creating rampant unemployment at a time when malaria, typhoid, tuberculosis and other illnesses had struck hard in the East. To help ease the burden, dime novels told tales of mountain men and fur trappers, scouts and bandits, and people in the East got lost in these stories. The sagas became a popular line of profit, fostering faith among the world-weary, many of whom had lost their farms or families.

Greeley began to advocate the message in his *New-York Tribune*, one of the nation's most popular newspapers. He saw the pluses from both sides: An individual could embrace the Jeffersonian principle and settle in a place where the terrain was inspiring,

PUSHING WEST
The most valuable land went to railroad companies (above), which turned around and sold the acreage for nearby farms and towns.

TALE TELLER
Editorials by Horace Greeley (far left) were picked up by many newspapers, shaping public opinion.

INDIAN LAND FOR SALE

GET A HOME
OF
YOUR OWN

❋

EASY PAYMENTS

PERFECT TITLE

❋

POSSESSION
WITHIN
THIRTY DAYS

FINE LANDS IN THE WEST
IRRIGATED
IRRIGABLE   GRAZING   AGRICULTURAL
DRY FARMING

In 1910 the Department of the Interior Sold Under Sealed Bids Allotted Indian Land as Follows :

Location.	Acres.	Average Price per Acre.	Location.	Acres.	Average Price per Acre.

Advertisement, Library of Congress.

HOSTILE TAKEOVER
The practice of boasting about the sale of Native lands continued well into the 20th century.

and businesses back East could handsomely profit by providing goods. As he once put it, "Every smoke that rises in the Great West marks a new customer to the counting rooms and warehouses of New York."

When the Republican government of Abraham Lincoln approved the Homestead Act in 1862 in the middle of the Civil War— without any opposition from the Southern states that had left the Union—it meant settlers could head out, find a piece of land of up to 160 acres, settle on it for free, work it for five years and then own it for $10. The promise seemed, on the surface, a deal unlike any other.

The rub, however, was getting out there, and then turning the dream into reality. That meant having enough money for equipment to travel, settle and farm. A wagon needed to be secured and packed, and one had to know what goods could be bought on the other end of the journey. And there was little knowledge of what else settlers would find when they arrived— other than, perhaps, Native Americans who might not be quite so amenable as the posters promised.

That was OK: Beyond the tales of marvels the dime novels promoted, manuals such as *The National Wagon Road Guide* offered their own wild-eyed encouragement, even suggesting that the ideas of arduous work and potential dangers along the way came only from a traveler's "fruitful imagination." That was what the men read; for the women, painfully little was mentioned about cooking and child care.

Getting Railroaded

But out many folks went, and when the various lines of the First Transcontinental Railroad were connected in 1869, passage itself became much easier. The railroad companies, needing more settlers to justify their great investment, created their own glorious posters, and used government land they bought for a song to bring towns along the route into existence.

"The railroad company takes a huge hand in trying to advertise the West because they want to populate it," says John Findlay, PhD, a professor of history at the University of Washington. "Every person they bring is going to pay a fare to get to and from the West. Once they produce crops, they're going to pay the railroad to ship them to market. They're going to win coming and going. And they also have enormous government land grants in return for running the rail line. The corporations are enormously powerful and when they show up and begin controlling things, the West is transformed dramatically."

The homesteaders, however, faced many hardships. They arrived out West to find the most fertile land had been co-opted by the rail companies, leaving them with rockier plots that were more difficult to farm. Bringing a family out West on the train was prohibitively expensive, so once you arrived, there was less money to get started. Historic drought was followed by historic rainfall, and then by even worse drought, running for 10 years starting in the mid-1880s. "Scientists" of the day promised that the more people toiled on the land, the more rain would somehow be called forth from the heavens. The very act of farming, authorities suggested, would bring rain (an idea that rail companies embraced). The challenges were such that many of the people who sought a new life on a farm or in a boomtown found themselves moving on or selling their land to a bigger business in order to have the funds to work it.

Those who managed to stay afloat could make use of a variety of new products. An invention called barbed wire easily corralled your farm animals. Proper digging equipment made finding well water possible, and setting up a windmill helped to distribute it properly.

But one machine never broke down: the one bringing people out West. Knowledge of gold and silver rushes—promoted by the press—brought other travelers seeking quick wealth. San Francisco companies invested heavily in real estate in the southern portion of California, betting correctly that a coming rail line in the 1880s would inspire the curious to explore what was then the dusty little town of Los Angeles. In time, 200,000 tourists came through on the strength of boosters and posters alone.

And that's what matters most to history. Without these calls for people to head past the Mississippi, there would be no West, wild or otherwise.

"All you have to do is look at a map," observes Richard White, PhD, a professor emeritus of history at Stanford University. "When you do, you see it takes Anglo-Americans about two-and-a-half centuries to get halfway across the continent. And then with the railroad, they get the rest of the way in less than a generation." ★

CHANGING LIVES
Abraham Lincoln's Homestead Act took effect the same day as the Emancipation Proclamation.

Western hero Kit Carson admitted to a lifetime of sorrow about the tragic fate of Ann White.

WORDS TO LIVE (AND DIE) BY

FAMOUS LETTERS, QUOTES, WITNESS ACCOUNTS AND MEMOIRS OFFER A RICH VIEW OF THE NOTORIOUS WEST.

FEW MOMENTS IN FILM CAPTURE the essence of the American West quite like the iconic line from the 1962 John Ford classic, *The Man Who Shot Liberty Valance*. "This is the West, sir," a reporter explains to James Stewart's Ransom Stoddard. "When the legend becomes fact, print the legend."

There has always been a big gray area between fact and legend in the colorful accounts of those wild days. Even the most dramatic stories about the period's famous names have been enhanced in the telling. Here are some of the greatest finds.

Kit Carson and the Death of Ann White

THE SCENE In late 1849, Carson, the incomparable mountain man and scout, had joined soldiers in a two-week pursuit of Utes and Apaches who had killed the entire party in a wagon train except for Mrs. Ann White, her baby daughter and a servant woman, whom they held captive. When the soldiers came upon the Indians, Carson urged the commander to charge; he refused, and the Indians killed White, and then fled. A discovery of one of White's belongings affected Carson greatly after her death.

THE SOURCE *Kit Carson's Own Story of His Life*

THE TEXT "[Mrs. White] evidently knew that someone was coming to her rescue. She did not see us, but it was apparent that she was endeavoring to make her escape when she received the fatal shot.... In camp was found a book [presumably the recently published, highly exaggerated dime novel *Kit Carson: Prince of the Gold Hunters*], the first of the kind I have ever seen, in which

BY THE BOOK
Carson wrote that Mrs. White "had not been killed more than five minutes" before being found.

I was made a great hero, slaying Indians by the hundred, and I have often thought that as Mrs. White would read the same, and knowing that I lived near, she would pray for my appearance and that she would be saved. I did come, but had not the power to convince those that were in command over me to pursue my plan for her rescue. I will say no more regarding the matter...."

Billy the Kid's Letters to Gov. Lew Wallace

THE SCENE The New Mexico territorial governor made a deal with William Bonney, aka Billy the Kid: Surrender and testify in a coming court case, and in turn receive amnesty. The Kid agreed, but then Wallace reneged. After several months, the wily Bonney escaped. Two years later, with Bonney convicted of killing Sheriff William Brady, he again sought Wallace's intervention. Receiving none, he escaped justice again. All of his letters to Wallace were respectful and intelligently delivered.

THE SOURCE Public record

THE TEXT "March 13, 1879: To his Excellency the Governor, General Lew Wallace; Dear Sir, I have heard that you will give $1,000 for my body which as I can understand it means alive as a witness." "March 20, 1879: Sir, I will keep the appointment I made but be sure and have men come that you can depend on. I am not afraid to die like a man fighting but I would not like to be killed like a dog unarmed." "March 4, 1881: I Expect you have forgotten what you promised me, this Month two years ago, but I have not and I think You had ought to have come and seen me as I requested you to.... I guess they mean to Send me up [to be hanged] without giving me any Show but they will have a nice

Gov. Lew Wallace at first denied offering Billy the Kid (inset) a pardon, but later changed his story.

Buffalo Bill was a legendary figure even before he created his Wild West show.

time doing it. I am not intirely [sic] without friends. I shall Expect to See you some time today. Patiently Waiting, I am truly Yours Respect—Wm. H. Bonney"

Buffalo Bill Kills His First Indian

THE SCENE While still a teen, Bill Cody, aka Buffalo Bill, took several jobs, among them as an unofficial Army scout helping guide troops to Utah, to support his family. It was here his exploits in the Utah War began.

THE SOURCE *True Tales of the Plains* by William F. Cody

THE TEXT "In front of me, and at the top of the high bank, I saw, against the moon, the head and high war bonnet of an Indian chief.

"The men ahead could not see him, but he had his gun leveled at them. I knew if he fired he could scarcely miss at that range. Some of my friends must be killed. I had halted at sight of him and he didn't see me. I had no time to think out the situation. I brought up my rifle and took what aim I could in the deceptive moonlight....

"The stillness of the river was split by a roar as the report echoed from bank to bank. Down tumbled the chief, over the edge, rolling over and over like a shot rabbit, till he landed plump in the water.... The proudest minute I'd ever known came [later] when Frank McCarthy swung me up on to his shoulder in the Fort Kearny barracks and announced to everybody there: 'Boys, Billy's downed his first Injun! And the kid couldn't have made a prettier job of it if he'd been a thirty-year scout!'"

John Wesley Hardin Kills Jim Smalley

THE SCENE Hardin, one of the most prolific gunmen in Wild West history, claimed to have killed 42 men. Arrested for one of those murders in January 1871, he was being escorted by Texas lawmen Edward Stakes and Jim Smalley to Waco for trial. On the way, with Stakes off getting food for the horses, Smalley began to beat and taunt Hardin—who'd bought a gun from a fellow prisoner before leaving with the officers.

THE SOURCE *The Life of John Wesley Hardin, Written By Himself*

THE TEXT "Capt. Stokes [sic] went to get some corn and fodder for our horses. While he was gone Jim Smelly [sic] cursed me, as was his habit, and threatened to shoot me, pointing his pistol at me to scare me. Then he sat down on a stump near our horses, which were hitched to the body of the tree. I pretended to be crying and got behind the little black pony. I put my head down on his back and meanwhile I untied the string that held my pistol. I kept one eye on him to see if he was watching me. When I got the pistol ready I rushed around on Jim and said: 'Throw up your hands.' He commenced to draw his pistol, when I fired and Jim Smelly fell dead, killed because he did not have sense enough to throw his hands at the point of a pistol."

Sitting Bull's Vision of the Battle of Little Bighorn

THE SCENE In the summer of 1875, a year before the event known as "Custer's Last Stand," Native forces of different tribes gathered for one great sun dance at the behest of Sitting Bull, the legendary Lakota leader. During the ceremony, Sitting Bull seemed to presage the U.S. Army massacre that would turn the tide against the Indians.

THE SOURCE *Sitting Bull: The Life of an American Patriot* by Robert M. Utley

THE TEXT "Sitting Bull approached the sun-dance lodge astride a magnificent black war horse.... He danced into the lodge and around the circle to the back then forward. He called out: 'I wish my friends to fill one pipe and I wish my people to fill one pipe.' Sitting Bull extended the pipes. 'I have nearly got them,' meaning his enemies, and he pantomimed drawing his enemies toward him. Then he swept his arms through the air and closed them over his chest. He had surrounded his enemies and had them in his power. Lifting the two pipes to the sky in offering, he declared, 'We have them. The Great Spirit has given our enemy into our power.' A song and dance of triumph and thanksgiving ended the ceremony. Sitting Bull intoned, 'The Great Spirit has given our enemies to us. We are to destroy them.'" ★

TRUTH & DARING Hardin (below left) once corrected his lengthy record of violence, writing, "I only killed one man for snoring."

LAKOTA LEADER Sitting Bull (below right) knew the importance of unity between the tribes.

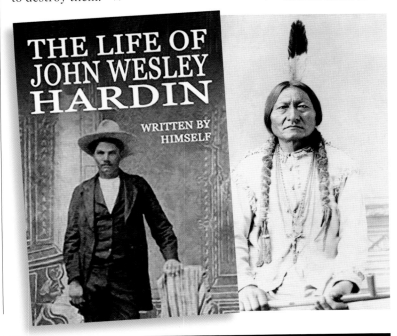

Notorious outlaw Jesse James was a legendary figure in the Wild West.

CHAPTER TWO

STRAIGHT SHOOTERS OF THE FRONTIER

Many images of Davy Crockett's Alamo bravery depict him in his trademark coonskin cap.

THE 10 SHOTS HEARD 'ROUND THE WEST

FROM THE ALAMO TO JESSE JAMES
AND THE DEATHS OF BUTCH AND SUNDANCE, HERE ARE
THE MURDEROUS MOMENTS THAT STILL RING LOUDEST.

FRONTIER FIGURE
Dime novels and
stage plays made
Davy Crockett (above)
a household name
in America.

DAVY CROCKETT AND THE ALAMO

DAY OF RECKONING March 6, 1836

THE LEAD-UP Crockett, the folk hero, U.S. representative from Tennessee and "King of the Wild Frontier," was famous for his exploits thanks in part to his exaggerated stories. After his 1835 defeat in Congress, he headed west to fight in the Texas Revolution alongside settlers hoping to win independence from the Mexican government. After years of skirmishes, Texans had captured the Alamo—a church, barracks and other small structures surrounded by a 10-foot wall in San Antonio—in October 1835. The Mexican Army was on its way, threatening to take the former mission back. Arriving at the Alamo in February 1836, Crockett raised the spirits of the troops—numbering only in the hundreds—through tall tales and fiddling.

THE MOMENT OF TRUTH The Mexican Army, led by Gen. Antonio López de Santa Anna, marched toward the mission with about 5,000 men and a determination that surprised the Texans. Sam Houston, general of the Texan Army, had sent Capt. Jim Bowie to the Alamo, telling the troops to abandon it; instead, Bowie, sick with tuberculosis, was convinced to remain and fight. Crockett helped keep the troops focused, but they were terribly outmatched. Santa Anna arrived and threatened to attack; Texan troops led by William Travis famously declared their intention to fight to "Victory or Death." The fighting began and within 90 minutes, many of the Texans were massacred. Crockett, one of the nation's most beloved figures, was among those killed; the bodies of the dead were burned beyond recognition.

WHY IT RESONATES Much like what happened later at the Battle of Little Bighorn, a stunning, embarrassing loss by outmatched U.S. troops inspired blood-thirsty vengeance. "Remember the Alamo!" became a rallying cry when Gen. Houston attacked and defeated Santa Anna a month and a half later. But the death of the exceedingly popular Crockett cemented the larger-than-life legend of a man who talked a good game about bravery and died a hero. Though the Alamo predates the Wild West period, many Westerns celebrated Crockett's feats, and the 1950s TV show, *Davy Crockett* starring Fess Parker, made coonskin caps the most-wanted holiday gift for boys everywhere.

JOSEPH SMITH

DAY OF RECKONING June 27, 1844

THE LEAD-UP In the annals of westward movement, the migration of the Mormons stands as an extraordinary, singular achievement. Smith, the church's founder, was a man of vision and visions—declaring, as a teenager in New York, that an angel had led him to a set of golden plates with hieroglyphics that, when translated, became the holy *Book of Mormon*. The book declared the eternal promise of America, and the site of Jesus' true church within. Founding The Church of Jesus Christ of Latter-day Saints, Smith built a religious empire that stressed community and economy. But outside their enclaves in Ohio and Missouri, neighbors felt threatened by the church's isolationist tendencies and power, and by Smith's growing ambitions. When he created an army, violence ensued and his followers were pushed out, moving to Illinois, where Smith built a huge temple and military force. He also began practicing polygamy and speaking of running for president. Splinter movements inside the church formed, along with complaints that Smith had too much control. Outside the church, anti-Mormon sentiment raged like an out-of-control fire.

THE MOMENT OF TRUTH When dissidents in the church criticized Smith, he excommunicated them, leading to the publication of a newspaper calling for reforms. After Smith approved the destruction of the paper itself, a riot ensued and Smith, fearing legal retribution, fled, but soon returned to face charges, and was held with his brother in a jail in Carthage, Illinois.

By then, tensions ran high, and an armed anti-Mormon mob stormed the jail. With Smith's brother killed instantly when he tried to keep out the mob, Smith, using a gun sneaked in to him before his imprisonment, wounded three before moving to jump out of the window. He was shot several times as he tried to escape and fell, mortally wounded, to the ground outside, where the mob kept on shooting him.

WHY IT RESONATES While the Tony-Award winning *Book of Mormon* musical poked fun at the religion, it currently counts more than 16 million followers worldwide, with Smith regarded as the Messianic martyr who started it all. After Smith's death, Brigham Young was elevated to head the church, and he shifted the operation to Utah, which remains its foundational center. The Mormon exodus was, wrote historian Richard W. Etulain, "better planned and more smoothly carried out than any other 19th-century westward movement."

TRUE BELIEVER
Joseph Smith (above) started the Mormon movement, maintaining an angel had led him to a book of golden plates that were inscribed with new scriptures, but he and his brother were killed by an anti-Mormon mob (top).

CUSTER'S LAST STAND

DAY OF RECKONING June 25, 1876

THE LEAD-UP Gen. George Armstrong Custer may have finished last in his class at West Point, but what he lacked in scholastics he more than made up for in both bravery and determination, which were bolstered by tremendous luck. Leading from the front in a series of surprise attacks and clad in uniforms that made him stand out during the Civil War—and bringing the press along to report on the battles—made his name loom large. After the Union victory, he wavered between politics and the military, fighting in the Indian Wars. In 1873, he discovered gold in South Dakota, which led to a rush and calls for the removal of the Native population from such rich land. Earlier skirmishes ultimately made fighting on the battleground along the Little Bighorn River in Montana a foregone conclusion for the U.S. troops.

THE MOMENT OF TRUTH An unprecedented number of Plains Indian tribes, angered by the "sell or else" threats of the U.S. government, gathered in large numbers in the area for a summer buffalo hunt, after an earlier sun-dance ceremony during which Chief Sitting Bull, in a vision, saw a historic victory over many soldiers. Neither Custer nor his fellow generals had a clue that thousands of warriors had convened in the area, and after sending Maj. Marcus Reno on an attack that proved ill-advised when countless Native forces suddenly appeared, a frustrated Custer made the remarkably rash decision to lead his troops into a typical quick-surprise attack in, of all things, broad daylight. They were met by thousands of Indian fighters who must have been shocked at their good fortune; in what historians have come to assume was pretty quick work, they annihilated Custer's forces. Word is that Oglala tribesman Joseph White Cow Bull ultimately shot and killed the famed general.

WHY IT RESONATES While President Ulysses S. Grant criticized Custer's poor battlefield strategy, the shocking death of one of the most popular and heroic military leaders in America moved the public to decry Indian savagery. It mattered little that the U.S. had done the attacking; the Indians now had to be destroyed. Little Bighorn stands as the turning point of policy toward the Native population, and it has barely wavered since.

LEGENDARY LEADER
As a cavalry leader during the Civil War, Gen. Custer (below) was nearly without peer, helping win a number of key battles. Despite the controversy of his Little Bighorn strategy (above right) his legacy remains heroic.

WILD BILL HICKOK

DAY OF RECKONING August 2, 1876
THE LEAD-UP Wild Bill had his day as the most famous and feared gunman and sometime peace officer in the West, ending up as the town marshal of Abilene, Kansas. But on October 5, 1871, while in a gun battle with Texas businessman Phil Coe, he accidentally shot and killed Mike Williams, one of his own deputies, which sent him into a personal and professional tailspin from which he would never recover. By 1876, having been diagnosed with glaucoma and living in the town of Deadwood, South Dakota, he was a compulsive gambler and marked man. On August 1, 1876, Jack McCall was in Deadwood's Nuttal & Mann's saloon; when a seat at a poker game became available, he joined in and promptly lost all his cash. Hickok, a fellow player at the table, offered to front McCall breakfast money for the next day and advised him not to play again until he could afford to.

THE MOMENT OF TRUTH The next day, a humiliated and drunk McCall stood at the bar, where Hickok was already gambling—and sitting, uncharacteristically, with his back to the door, unprotected. Seeing an opportunity to avenge the perceived insult, McCall produced a .45-caliber revolver, shouted, "Damn you, take that!" and put two bullets into the back of the head of the legendary Hickok. When asked later why he hadn't faced Hickok like a man, McCall reportedly answered, "I didn't want to commit suicide." It took two trials to convict McCall but on March 1, 1877, he was hanged.

WHY IT RESONATES It was the moment when the Wild West truly became a place where a hard man was destined to die the way he lived. It would be difficult to imagine a life more ready-made for a complete Hollywood production, and it's no surprise that only a portion of the films devoted to Hickok's many adventures also include the ending, focusing instead on retelling ever-taller tales of Wild Bill's life.

COWARDLY CULPRIT
Jack McCall (top) was hanged for killing Hickok (above), and reportedly buried with the noose still around his neck.

TV'S TAKE
On *Deadwood*, Keith Carradine (below left) was cast as Wild Bill; Timothy Olyphant (below) played Sheriff Seth Bullock.

BAD BOY
Billy the Kid (right) killed eight men before his death at age 21, but his legend grew thanks to news of his violent exploits.

BOUNTY HUNTER
It took a year for Pat Garrett (below) to collect the $500 reward for killing Billy.

BILLY THE KID

DAY OF RECKONING July 14, 1881

THE LEAD-UP William Bonney, aka Billy the Kid, may not have been the most prolific killer in the West, but he was the most mysterious and among the meanest. Being small in stature subjected him to frequent insults, which he often resolved with his trusty firearm. But the one killing that followed him to the end came in April 1878, with the shooting of Sheriff William Brady in the New Mexico territory during the infamous Lincoln County War. With two factions fighting for power in the area, Bonney, in support of the Regulators, killed Brady, whose efforts for James Dolan's group led to the killing of Billy's boss. Brady's death put Sheriff Pat Garrett on the case to root out and kill Billy the Kid.

THE MOMENT OF TRUTH After tracking the Kid for eight months—which included one arrest and an escape—Garrett finally heard that he was staying at the home of Pete Maxwell. He visited Maxwell late one night. The Kid awoke and entered the dark room where Garrett was talking to Maxwell. As Garrett later recalled, "The intruder came close, leaned both hands on the bed, his right hand almost touching my knee, and asked, in a low tone: 'Who are they, Pete?'...The Kid must have felt [my] presence and raised his pistol.... Quickly I drew my revolver and fired, threw my body aside, and fired again. The second shot was useless; the Kid fell dead and was with his many victims."

WHY IT RESONATES No one was ever sure of the Kid's real name, and only one photo of him exists. The mystery of his life and lore of his death has fascinated generations, and he stands forever in films, song and newspaper accounts as the quintessential outlaw.

THE GUNFIGHT AT THE O.K. CORRAL

DAY OF RECKONING October 26, 1881

THE LEAD-UP What exactly led to this most infamous confrontation? Start with two frustrated, ambitious factions. On the one hand, you had a band of cattle rustlers who'd long been used to getting away with petty criminal activity in and around Tombstone, Arizona; the group included Billy Claiborne and two sets of brothers, Ike and Billy Clanton, and Tom and Frank McLaury. And then there was a group of politically minded lawmen and businessmen seeking their own fortunes in town, including brothers Virgil, Wyatt and Morgan Earp, along with Doc Holliday. Their bitterness grew to a head thanks to broken agreements and stagecoach robberies, increased town anger about the Clantons' activities, and the Earps' desire to be seen as the conduits of order. And, like many a Wild West feud, the Clantons being Southerners and the Earps having fought for the Union during the Civil War didn't help.

THE MOMENT OF TRUTH Virgil Earp, the town marshal, deputized his brothers and Holliday when tensions boiled to the point where a shootout became a certainty. (Among other things, Wyatt had argued with Tom McLaury the night before and smacked him in the head with his pistol.) The nine combatants finally met in a vacant lot on Fremont Street not far from the corral in question. The shooting was fierce but quick; after 30 seconds, Billy Clanton and both McLaury brothers lay dead, Virgil and Morgan Earp were wounded, Ike Clanton and Billy Claiborne escaped, Holliday was barely grazed and the most famous name among them, Wyatt Earp, was unharmed. A little more than a month later, a hearing found that the Earps and Holliday had acted within the law. When vendettas soon left Virgil shot and Morgan dead, Wyatt Earp went on a tear of retribution that helped make his name.

WHY IT RESONATES It took Stuart Lake's 1931 biography of Wyatt Earp to truly sound the clarion call on this event. Then, John Ford's brilliant 1946 film *My Darling Clementine* and the 1957 Burt Lancaster-Kirk Douglas classic, *Gunfight at the O.K. Corral*, added the power of fiction—geographic and otherwise—that made this the most mythologized event of the notorious West. Good guys, bad guys, friendship and firearms have proved to be a powerful combination ever since.

O.K. CORRAL
Seven months after the gunfight took place near here (top), a fire damaged the famed spot (this view is from Fremont Street).

DYNAMIC DUO
Doc Holliday (above left) became friends with Wyatt Earp (above right) after saving his life once in Texas.

WHERE JESSE JAMES WAS KILLED

DEADLY DEPARTED
Rumors had it that Jesse James wasn't actually killed at his St. Joseph house; his corpse (above) proved them wrong.

FAIR-WEATHER FRIEND
After killing James in his home (top), Robert Ford was convicted of his murder—and pardoned that same day.

JESSE JAMES

DAY OF RECKONING April 3, 1882

THE LEAD-UP Frank James and his younger but more hard-nosed brother, Jesse, found success in a long series of murderous bank robberies. In addition, Jesse's portrayal in some newspapers as a fighter for Southern values in a post-Civil War America made him something of an odd folk hero. But in 1876, the James-Younger Gang (which included Cole Younger and his three brothers) attempted what proved to be a disastrous raid on the First National Bank of Northfield, Minnesota; after that, the James brothers were on the run. To keep their whereabouts secret, they put their trust in two onetime members of their gang: the brothers Charley and Robert Ford, who moved into Jesse's home in St. Joseph, Missouri, with Jesse going by an alias.

THE MOMENT OF TRUTH In early 1882, Missouri governor Thomas Crittenden promised a bounty of $10,000 for help in the capture of Jesse James, a figure that inspired Robert Ford to make a secret deal.

On that fateful morning, reports in the newspaper made Jesse suspicious of Ford, but not enough to outright accuse him. Still, as Ford would later say in his legal account, "I knew I had not fooled him; he was too sharp for that." When Jesse took off his gun belt and climbed on a chair in the living room to dust a framed picture, Ford saw his destiny unfold. "It came to me suddenly, 'Now or never is your chance.' Without further thought or a moment's delay I pulled my revolver and leveled it as I sat. [Jesse] heard the hammer click as I cocked it with my thumb and started to turn as I pulled the trigger. The ball struck him just behind the ear and he fell like a log, dead."

WHY IT RESONATES The fact that Jesse James engineered the first-ever peacetime armed bank robbery makes his life fodder for a variety of pop-culture history. Add to that the fact that Ford was condemned by the public for so cowardly an act against a popular figure, and it also speaks volumes about the West's reputation as a place where audacity, no matter the circumstances, was admired.

SITTING BULL

DAY OF RECKONING December 15, 1890

THE LEAD-UP The influence of the great Hunkpapa Sioux medicine man and military leader would be hard to quantify; he was tactical, philosophical, inspirational and irreversible. When other Native leaders compromised with whites, he derisively declared they were "fools to make yourselves slaves to a piece of fat bacon, some hard-tack and a little sugar and coffee." The man whose visions foresaw the victory at Little Bighorn did not surrender until 1881, and then, after a short stint in Buffalo Bill's Wild West shows and a friendship with Annie Oakley, he remained a feared thorn in the side of U.S. forces, sequestered at the Standing Rock Sioux Agency reservation in the Dakotas. Ever-defiant of calls for him to lead his community of Plains Indians to compromise, he said of the American whites: "Possession is a disease with them."

THE MOMENT OF TRUTH Federal Indian Service Agent James McLaughlin, who wanted Native peoples to assimilate and accept their new roles as farmers, even though the land on the reservation made farming incredibly challenging, had long been at odds with Sitting Bull. In the ensuing frustration, a burst of visionary fervor from a shaman in the region birthed the Ghost Dance movement, which suggested that a life of gatherings and meditation would lead to control of the lands being returned. When Sitting Bull embraced the movement, and added a threat of confrontation, McLaughlin saw great trouble on the horizon and ordered his arrest. Expecting soldiers at his door, Sitting Bull instead found Lakota Sioux reservation police. "We are of the same blood," he told them. "If the white men want me to die, they ought not to put up the Indians to kill me." But a scuffle soon broke out and as supporters of the chief tried to protect him, Sioux police officers put two bullets into the side of Sitting Bull's head.

WHY IT RESONATES Growing terror about the Ghost Dance movement brought troops to nearby Wounded Knee two weeks after Sitting Bull's murder. The ensuing massacre of 300 Native men, women and children made clear the U.S. government's unwavering plans for manifest destiny in the West. But with each decade, Sitting Bull's reputation, as a symbol of the power of principle and the necessity of resistance, has grown.

95 The Detroit Free Press **EXTRA**

DETROIT, MONDAY, DECEMBER 15, 1890

CHIEF SITTING BULL KILLED

Chief Who Lead Sioux In Battle of the Little Big Horn Is Shot By Indian Police When His Warriors Try to Stop His Arrest At His Village On Grand River

Chief Sitting Bull was shot to death today after his warriors tried to prevent his arrest by Indian Police. Eight Indians, including Sitting Bull's son, Crowfoot, were also killed, as were six of the police. After the battle of the

Little Big Horn, Sitting Bull escaped to Canada, but returned to the United States after being promised a pardon. He then appeared in Buffalo Bill's Wild West Show, but lately he has been urging the Sioux not to sell their lands.

Since Sitting Bull's return to the U.S. the strange religious craze of the Ghost Dance has spread among the Indians, who believe that a Messiah is coming to free them from the oppression of the white man.

Chief Sitting Bull

See Scoop No. 96.— GERONIMO SURRENDERS TO GEN. MILES

STANDING STRONG
Sitting Bull (above) led many tribes and opposed all treaties that aimed to remove Indians from their homelands.

CHANGE AGENT
Despite his handling of Sitting Bull, James McLaughlin (below) titled his memoir, *My Friend the Indian.*

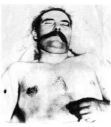

A HARD MAN
John Wayne (top) based his final role on Hardin. The outlaw (above), died at the hands of John Selman, who put a slug into the back of his head.

JOHN WESLEY HARDIN

DAY OF RECKONING August 19, 1895

THE LEAD-UP Hardin is generally regarded as the most ruthless gunman of his day. Unlike the more notorious Jesse James and Billy the Kid, however, Wesley Hardin didn't have the same yarn-spinning support from newspapermen and dime novelists. What he did have was a hair-trigger temper and a long-held grudge against anti-slavery Union forces, seemingly forged through political life in Texas and some early personal tragedy. Hardin's rap sheet began with him stabbing a fellow student who'd taunted him at age 14, continued to his killing one of his uncle's former slaves and included once shooting an Indian "for practice." In all, he shot and killed somewhere between 20 and 40 victims, including one who snored too loudly. Escaping the law and living in Florida under an assumed name, Hardin was captured on a train heading back to Pensacola from Alabama. Texas Ranger John Armstrong entered Hardin's rail compartment; when the outlaw reached for his gun he found it stuck in his suspenders. That gave Armstrong time to club him until he was knocked out. Tried in June 1878, Hardin was sentenced to 25 years in prison. During the 17 years he served, he studied law and wrote one of the most extraordinary autobiographies of the period.

THE MOMENT OF TRUTH Released in 1894, Hardin found life on the outside unkind. His beloved wife had died while he was in prison and he ended up in El Paso, Texas, with few prospects for a legal career, but with two prominent enemies—peace officer John Selman and his son John Selman Jr. When Hardin's then-girlfriend was arrested by Selman Jr., Hardin threatened to kill them both. Later that day, Hardin was shooting dice in a bar when Selman entered and put a slug into the back of Hardin's head. Though the outlaw was dead, Selman shot him twice more for good measure.

WHY IT RESONATES As Western history continues to be revised, and as society's obsession with psychotic killers grows, the man historian Howard R. Lamar, PhD, called "the greatest killer of them all" only grows in stature. His autobiography remains a classic, and John Wayne's character in his final film, *The Shootist*, is loosely based on Hardin.

BUTCH CASSIDY AND THE SUNDANCE KID

DAY OF RECKONING November 7, 1908
THE LEAD-UP The last of the great robbers of the Wild West, Utah-born Robert LeRoy Parker quickly eschewed his Mormon parents' ways and fell happily under the influence of a horse thief named Mike Cassidy. After an apprenticeship robbing banks with the notorious McCarty brothers, buying a ranch in Hole-in-the-Wall, Wyoming, and serving 18 months for thievery, Parker emerged from jail as Butch Cassidy (the last name in tribute to his mentor). In 1896, Cassidy formed the Wild Bunch gang, which included the man who became his closest associate, Harry Longabaugh, whose nickname came from his stint in the Sundance, Wyoming, prison. Butch was an affable leader, and the gang robbed banks and trains until heat from railroad companies pushed them to South America with Sundance's girl, Etta Place. The outlaws seesawed between mining and robbing, and remained in hiding.

THE MOMENT OF TRUTH In early November 1908, two masked bandits stole a mule train carrying the payroll for a silver mine in Southern Bolivia. Three days later, Butch and Sundance were at a boardinghouse; the owner recognized one of the mules with the mine's brand. He alerted authorities, and soldiers surrounded the house. Most of the pair's guns and ammo were outside with the mules. When Sundance made a run for them, he was hit several times; Butch was also shot trying to pull him to safety. Sundance's wounds were serious and the end was near. Putting his friend out of his misery, Cassidy shot the Kid in the head, then put a fatal bullet into his own. In the morning, the bandits were identified as the robbers and reportedly buried in an unmarked grave in nearby San Vicente cemetery.

WHY IT RESONATES Or...did it really happen that way? Like Jesus and Elvis, Butch Cassidy and the Sundance Kid were believed to have survived, with friends and family later reporting that they'd seen each even decades later. Given the myth-making of the Wild West, it would be hard to come up with a better "end" for the duo. ★

THE WILD BUNCH
Cassidy's gang included (above from left) the Sundance Kid, Will Carver, Ben Kilpatrick, Harvey Logan and Butch Cassidy.

HOLLYWOOD HEROES
Robert Redford (below left) and Paul Newman (below right) brought humor and a restless spirit to Butch and Sundance's lives in their 1969 film, *Butch Cassidy and the Sundance Kid*.

THE DEADLY YEARS

The dark times between 1880 and 1882 set a high mark for frontier retributions.

As ignominious achievements go, it's hard to argue against the years 1880 to 1882 being an apex of violence in the Wild West, even by frontier standards. The shootings of Billy the Kid and Jesse James, and the Gunfight at the O.K. Corral, all occurred during this period, and between vendettas related to those events and other random acts, you get a series of killings that would later inflame Hollywood's imagination.

It says a lot that, for instance, that on March 2, 1880, salesman James Moorehead was killed in a Las Vegas, New Mexico, hotel because his waiter, James Allen, didn't like the supposedly sarcastic way he ordered eggs. ("A Waiter's Wrath" was the next day's newspaper headline.) But by then, the same town had already seen the January 22 Variety Hall shootout, which found assistant marshal "Mysterious" Dave Mather reacting to the sudden shooting death of his boss, Marshal Joe Carson, by four rowdy cowboys by killing one, gravely injuring a second and wounding the other two.

While that year closed out with famed Sheriff Pat Garrett's men dispatching two associates of Billy the Kid's—Tom O'Folliard and Charlie Bowdre —spring came in like a lion in 1881 with one of the most notoriously named gunfights in Western history: April 14's Four Dead in Five Seconds shootout. An extremely divisive court case involving murdered Mexican *vaqueros* (cowboys) and Texas cattle rustlers created a powder keg of tension, and El Paso's marshal Dallas Stoudenmire, who was known to shoot first and ask questions later, found himself in the middle of it when he heard a gunshot that afternoon. A constable in the case, Gus Krempkau, had been shot; Stoudenmire followed the sound across the street and first killed an innocent bystander, followed by a friend of the man who'd shot Krempkau. Then Krempkau killed the shooter before dying soon after. Did it all take more than five seconds? Sure, but the name struck a resounding chord.

Then, in the wake of the O.K. Corral shootout, Virgil Earp was maimed by gunfire in an ambush on December 28, 1881, and his brother Morgan was killed the following March. So Wyatt Earp gathered a posse and exacted revenge on the Cowboys gang responsible for the attacks on his brothers. One evening, the posse came upon nine members of the Cowboys, fronted by William "Curly Bill" Brocius, a prime suspect in Morgan's murder. Brocius reportedly fired at Wyatt and missed; Earp then killed Brocius with a single shot to the chest. The exchange was followed by a volley of bullets; nobody else was felled except a horse.

The spate of killings exposed the breadth of violence during the wildest part of the period. "Most of the murders in the West are going to be from ambush of one kind or another and then we have this small residue, which is either someone is drunk, or one person is simply taking full advantage," says Richard White, PhD, a professor emeritus of history at Stanford University. "But when you have two guys actually facing each other? Those are just vanishingly few. And that's one of the reasons they become classic."

PRIME SUSPECT
William "Curly Bill" Brocius (opposite page) had once been protected from a lynch mob by Wyatt Earp, who later killed him after his brother Morgan Earp's death.

MEAN MARSHAL
A year and a half after his most famous gunfight, Dallas Stoudenmire (left) himself was shot and killed.

Orphaned at a young age, Calamity Jane learned to rely on her wits and strength in her storied life.

LADIES OF LEGEND

GAMBLERS AND GUN-TOTERS, MADAMS AND MOLLS—THE PLAINS PRODUCED SOME REMARKABLE WOMEN WHO STOOD OUT FOR THEIR BEAUTY AND BRAWN.

LOTTIE DENO
(1844–1934)

OCCUPATION Gambler, murderer's moll, Sunday-school teacher

HER STORY The "Deno" in Carlotta Thompkins' nickname is short for "dinero," the Spanish word for money, and Lottie Deno earned a ton of it in her time as one of the most famous and successful professional poker players in the Southwest. Learning the trade from her father, she came to San Antonio at age 21, where she earned her chips and fell for fellow gambler Frank Thurmond. When Thurmond was accused of murder, they both went on the lam for years, during which time Deno secured her reputation at the tables (*Gunsmoke*'s Miss Kitty is based on her). She and Thurmond married in 1880, moved to Deming, New Mexico, and quit the game; Thurmond worked at the local bank and Deno co-founded the town's Episcopal Church.

LAURA BULLION
(1876–1961)

OCCUPATION Outlaw, prostitute, seamstress

HER STORY As one of the female outlaws working in Butch Cassidy's cagey gang of train robbers, she was known as the "Rose of the Wild Bunch." But the thorns were infamous as well. As one detective sized things up: "I wouldn't think helping hold up a train was too much for her. She is cool, shows absolutely no fear and in male attire would readily pass for a boy." In the company of her boyfriend/fellow gang member, Ben "The Tall Texan" Kilpatrick, she tried to evade the law after the infamous Great Northern train robbery, but ended up serving three years in jail before fading into obscurity.

BIG NOSE KATE HORONY
(1850-1940)

OCCUPATION Prostitute, bakery owner, companion to Doc Holliday

HER STORY The Wild West tale of Doc Holliday's longtime companion begins when Horony, who came to America from Hungary as a baby, left her foster home at 16 and stowed away on a riverboat to St. Louis. Entering a convent at 19 and a brothel at 20, she met Holliday in Texas in 1877, which was the beginning of a tempestuous relationship. After they traveled to Tombstone together, she worked as a prostitute while Holliday tried his hand at the gambling tables. Did she see the Gunfight at the O.K. Corral from the window of the local boardinghouse, as she later claimed? Perhaps; what is known is that she was married for a time to blacksmith George Cummings after Holliday's death, moved to Arizona and lived to age 90.

ANNIE OAKLEY
(1860-1926)

OCCUPATION Trapper, shooter, hunter, Buffalo Bill's Wild West show star

HER STORY The greatest sharpshooter of them all started honing her skills at age 8, and by 15 she famously beat top marksman Frank Butler in an 1875 shooting match, winning both the top prize and Butler's heart. (The two would share a 50-year marriage.) She joined Buffalo Bill's touring show in 1885 and became the most beloved female star of her day, hitting dimes tossed into the air and putting out candles with the whiz of her bullets. A train crash and a car accident left her with considerable injuries, but she managed to make a comeback. Sitting Bull joined Buffalo Bill's company for a time primarily due to his admiration for the lady he called "Little Sure Shot." After Oakley died from anemia, an inconsolable Butler followed 18 days later.

PEARL HART
(1876-1955)

OCCUPATION Cook, singer, stagecoach robber, cigar-store manager

HER STORY Early life was hardly rosy for Hart. She'd married an abusive alcoholic but left him and headed for Colorado. "I was only 22, good-looking, desperate, discouraged and ready for anything that might come," she later said. "Anything," it turned out, included notoriety as the last of the female stagecoach robbers, a crime she committed in 1899. Sentenced to five years, she was later pardoned, with some guessing a pregnancy that would have embarrassed the state. After that, Hart married and faded into obscurity, becoming a fixture in tales of the Old West.

POKER ALICE IVERS
(1851-1930)

OCCUPATION Gambler, brothel owner, rancher

HER STORY "Praise the lord and place your bets. I'll take your money with no regrets." Thus spoke British-born Alice Ivers, who dealt the hands and scooped up the chips during a successful career at tables throughout Colorado and New Mexico. After marrying Colorado mining engineer Frank Duffield, she'd tag along to his many poker games; when Duffield died in a mining explosion, Ivers took up the game and won the modern equivalent of hundreds of thousands of dollars, while keeping her trusty .38 around to end disagreements. Three times a widow (she supposedly married the third time instead of paying the man the debt she owed), Ivers was the inspiration for the 1987 TV movie *Poker Alice*, in which she was played by another legend: Elizabeth Taylor.

ETTA PLACE
(1878-UNKNOWN)

OCCUPATION Outlaw

HER STORY The gorgeous companion of Harry Longabaugh, aka the Sundance Kid, was, according to the Pinkerton Detective agents, a woman of "classic good looks, 5-foot-4...weighing between 110 and 120 pounds with a medium build and brown hair." Little is known of her, yet what feeds the mystery is the photo she and Sundance took just before the pair and Butch Cassidy went to Buenos Aires to escape the law. The trio lived on a ranch in Argentina and left for occasional stateside visits and one 1904 bank robbery. After tiring of the outlaw life and leaving Longabaugh in San Francisco in 1906, the trail runs cold. She lives forever in Katharine Ross' performance in *Butch Cassidy and the Sundance Kid*.

CALAMITY JANE CANNARY

(1852-1903)

OCCUPATION Scout, frontierswoman, dance-hall girl, prostitute, sharpshooter

HER STORY Among the greatest legends of her day, Jane was known for spinning tales in Buffalo Bill's Wild West shows, wearing men's clothes and maintaining a fascinating obsession with Wild Bill Hickok. The oldest of six orphaned siblings, she began, at 14, helping to care for the family; she said it was while working as a scout that she earned her nickname, courtesy of a military captain whom she'd saved from calamity. Or was it because she told men that offending her meant courting calamity? She married twice, claimed to have wed Hickok (she is buried beside him), supposedly had at least two daughters and found any happiness sadly undone by a lifelong struggle with alcohol.

MARY FIELDS

(C.1832-1914)

OCCUPATION Domestic postal carrier, cook, freight hauler, farmer, building forewoman

HER STORY The first African American woman to work for the U.S. Postal Service, she delivered mail via stagecoach, starting around age 60. By then, Fields had spent years at the side of her benefactress, a convent mother superior, earning a reputation for a kind heart and a mean punch. Among her admirers: fellow Montanan Gary Cooper, who in a 1959 tribute in *Ebony,* wrote that "Stagecoach Mary" was "one of the freest souls ever to draw a breath, or a .38." ★

Detectives described the blue-eyed Butch (left) as being wanted for crimes in Wyoming, Utah, Idaho and other states. They called Sundance (right) an escaped fugitive who liked to wear his hair in a pompadour.

PARDNERS
ON THE PLAINS

BUTCH AND SUNDANCE, WYATT EARP AND
DOC HOLLIDAY—THE WEST WOULD NEVER HAVE BEEN
WON WITHOUT ITS MOST FAMOUS TEAM PLAYERS.

How did Wyatt Earp describe his fast-draw friendship with his closest pal Doc Holliday? "I found him a loyal friend and good company. He was a dentist whom necessity had made a gambler; a gentleman whom disease had made a vagabond; a philosopher whom life had made a caustic wit; a long, lean blond fellow nearly dead with consumption and at the same time the most skillful gambler and nerviest, speediest, deadliest man with a six-gun I ever knew."

OK...granted, this florid prose actually came from the pen (and mind) of Earp's biographer Stuart Lake, but one need not doubt the veracity of Earp's emotion and loyalty to his O.K. Corral compatriot. These pals, whose bond has been cemented by many a Hollywood portrayal, are hardly the only pair of aces in frontier history. Here are the partnerships that still live on in lore.

FRANK AND JESSE JAMES

FRONTIER CRED Frank was older by four years, and lived 33 years longer than his more notorious brother. But together, between 1866 and 1876, they were a criminal sensation, committing murder and causing mayhem (not to mention withdrawing thousands of dollars) with their successful armed bank robberies.

SQUAD GOALS The pair, along with the Younger Gang, were distinguished by their audacity, robbing a bank while a political rally was underway nearby, and burgling the box office at a Kansas City fair in the middle of a crowd. An 1876 Minnesota bank robbery gone bad left Frank and Jesse on the run.

HOW THINGS ENDED Violently for Jesse, in April 1882, when he was shot by newer gang recruit Robert Ford. Five months later, Frank turned himself in, saying, "For 21 years...I have never known a day of perfect peace." Ultimately acquitted of his crimes, he did odd jobs for decades, including working the door at a St. Louis burlesque theater where patrons were told they could "Come get your ticket purchased [from] the legendary Frank James."

BAD BROS
Frank (top) and Jesse (above) were fodder for dime novels—until the books were banned.

BUTCH CASSIDY AND THE SUNDANCE KID

FRONTIER CRED The top-billed duo of a loose band of outlaws known as the Wild Bunch, they were immortalized in the 1969 Oscar-winning movie bearing their names. While there's no word on how the two met, their bond extended to their escape (along with Sundance's girl, Etta Place) from the U.S., and the law, on February 20, 1901, followed by a second act ranching and doing some more robbing in South America.

SQUAD GOALS They were experts at stealing from trains, stagecoaches and banks, and also for being quick with their guns. (Unlike the rest of the gang, Butch and Sundance used theirs more for threats than deaths.) A June 2, 1899, Union Pacific Railroad robbery netted between $30,000 and $60,000. It was one of many jobs that earned them the attention of the Pinkerton Detective Agency.

HOW THINGS ENDED Mysteriously—Butch and Sundance supposedly died after a November 7, 1908, gun battle in Bolivia, although the bodies were never positively identified.

WYATT EARP AND DOC HOLLIDAY

FRONTIER CRED Wyatt, Virgil and Morgan Earp and Wyatt's best bud, Doc Holliday, gambled at the tables in Tombstone, Arizona, and with their lives at the famed Gunfight at the O.K. Corral. Wyatt and Doc had met in Texas, where Doc saved the lawman's life during the Indian Wars in the mid-1870s.

SQUAD GOALS In the years leading up to the O.K. Corral battle, the ambition for Earp and the others had been to gain a footing ruling Tombstone. The killings interrupted the plan, and Earp and Holliday headed to New Mexico.

HOW THINGS ENDED Prematurely, due to Holliday's death from tuberculosis. Also, Earp reportedly took issue with an anti-Semitic slur Holliday delivered (Earp's common-law wife was Jewish). But a year later, Earp worked on his friend's behalf as he faced criminal charges. Holliday passed away in 1887 at 36. It would take a month for his onetime best friend to hear the news.

Wyatt Earp (seated) was no stranger to gunplay; one outlaw called Holliday's (above left) temper "ungovernable."

OLIVER WINCHESTER AND B. TYLER HENRY

FRONTIER CRED The ultimate firearms fighters worked together, competed against each other and ultimately produced the rifles that ruled the West. The popular Henry rifle, designed in 1860, was favored for its .44-caliber cartridge, 16-shot swift lever action and no leak of burning powder gas. Winchester, a successful businessman who had taken over the failing Smith & Wesson company, hired the brilliant Henry and made a mint.

SQUAD GOALS Winchester bought out competitors and used the talents of the engineers under him to mold the Henry rifle into the Winchester model, which added an improved magazine and wooden fore-end. In 1873, the company released the Winchester '73, the most popular rifle of its era.

HOW THINGS ENDED Litigiously, with Henry suing Winchester in 1866 for more control and compensation, and his boss reorganizing his business as the Winchester Repeating Arms Company and working from Henry's patents. Henry left and died in 1898, having created the template for one of America's most popular and reliable weapons.

GUN RUNNERS Winchester (top left) owned the New Haven Arms Company that produced Henry's (top right) famed rifle.

EXPLORERS Spending 20 years as a scout served Carson (standing, right) well when it came to guiding Frémont (seated).

KIT CARSON AND JOHN C. FRÉMONT

FRONTIER CRED Frémont, a topographical engineer, was the "Great Pathfinder" of the West, thanks to his detailed exploration of the Oregon Trail in the 1840s. He never would have succeeded had he not chanced upon Carson, an incomparable mountain man, on a Missouri River steamboat. Frémont's respect for Carson was reflected in his published land surveys, leading to Carson being the famed subject of dime novels.

SQUAD GOALS Frémont's attention to detail—latitudes and longitudes, elevations, plant and animal life and information on water and pasture grass—fueled the government's determination to open the West. Carson's daring, including the two days he hunted Indians who had ambushed a group of travelers, were the stuff of heroics. When Frémont trampled one Indian who was set to attack Carson, the mountain man felt he owed the engineer his life.

HOW THINGS ENDED Loyally, with the pair parting ways after their shared service in the Mexican-American War. Carson delivered Frémont's military papers to Washington in what the engineer called "a service of great trust, honor and danger."

LELAND STANFORD, COLLIS POTTER HUNTINGTON, MARK HOPKINS AND CHARLES CROCKER

FRONTIER CRED The "Big Four" were known more for their size than stature, but they founded the Central Pacific Railroad, one of the first exceedingly rich corporations out West. All four originally came in search of gold and discovered that the real money lay in building railroads and selling supplies to forty-niners. Innovative engineer Theodore Judah called the four together and sold them on the train idea. When Judah died unexpectedly, the four held all the plans.

SQUAD GOALS Crocker ran construction, Hopkins kept the books, Huntington handled supplies and Stanford lobbied Washington, and was soon elected California governor. They weren't close, but they quickly learned the path to profit in railroads was through government subsidies for land.

HOW THINGS ENDED Profitably, as 15,000 workers (mostly Chinese immigrants) helped build the First Transcontinental Railroad, heading east from Sacramento, connecting with the Union Pacific in Utah in 1869.

RAILROAD BARONS
Clockwise, from top left: Edwin Crocker, Huntington, Stanford, Hopkins and Charles Crocker got rich off the Central Pacific Railroad.

F SITTING BULL
SIOUX —

Sitting Bull eventually fled to Canada but Crazy Horse (bottom right) kept fighting until his May 6, 1877, surrender.

SITTING BULL AND CRAZY HORSE

FRONTIER CRED There was always respect between Crazy Horse, the brave Oglala Sioux military leader, and Sitting Bull, the famed Hunkpapa Lakota medicine man. But the pair never truly came together until the Battle of Little Bighorn, aka Custer's Last Stand.

SQUAD GOALS The War Department had declared that on January 1, 1876, all Indian tribes were required to return to their reservations, an order Crazy Horse ignored. By that June, he was winning a Plains battle against Gen. George Crook on the strength of his vexing strategies. Already aware of Sitting Bull's visions of a great victory over more soldiers, Crazy Horse brought his troops to his fellow leader's side in late June, just in time for an American attack led by an overmatched Gen. George Custer. Crazy Horse and Sitting Bull won the day.

HOW THINGS ENDED Violently, as Little Bighorn led to a clearing out of all "hostiles" by the government. Both Indian leaders met vicious ends, yet remain symbols of resistance even today.

BILLY THE KID AND TOM O'FOLLIARD

FRONTIER CRED O'Folliard was a young Texas cattle rustler who came to New Mexico in the late 1870s to fight in the skirmish-filled Lincoln County War. He met William "Billy the Kid" Bonney and the two quickly became best friends. When the war ended, O'Folliard was second in command of Billy's gang.

SQUAD GOALS The gang's involvement in violent incidents in the 1870s plays like a brief but bloody rap sheet. It all spurred lawman Pat Garrett's pursuit of the crew.

HOW THINGS ENDED Inevitably, as Billy, O'Folliard and the others rode into New Sumner, New Mexico, on December 19, 1880, where Garrett and a posse lay in wait. Garrett shot O'Folliard in the chest; reportedly, it took 45 minutes for him to die after Garrett refused to put him out of his misery. The following July, Garrett killed the Kid. The best friends, along with fellow outlaw Charlie Bowdre, are buried together in Fort Sumner; the grave marker identifies them as "PALS."

CHARLES GOODNIGHT AND OLIVER LOVING

FRONTIER CRED There's no denying the resemblance between the characters Woodrow Call and Augustus McCrae and history's greatest cattlemen pair, Goodnight and Loving, in the Lonesome Dove miniseries, based on the books by Larry McMurtry—with Tommy Lee Jones and Robert Duvall playing the duo.

SQUAD GOALS The pair formed their partnership in June 1866. The Goodnight-Loving Trail they ultimately forged using 2,000 head of cattle began in southern Texas, headed up through New Mexico toward Denver, and then continued up to Wyoming. In time, it became among the most famously well-traveled and profitable trails in the decades of the runs.

HOW THINGS ENDED Separately but tragically. Loving died after fighting off a band of Comanches who attacked him on the trail to New Mexico in 1867. Goodnight continued to extend trails throughout the region, eventually settling in as a Texas rancher who became a pioneer in cattle breeding. He died in 1929 at a small ranch near Goodnight, a Texas panhandle town named for him. ★

BEST FRIENDS
Billy the Kid (top left) and O'Folliard (top right) spent years rustling cattle and causing mayhem before they were killed.

CATTLE CREW
Songs, streets, awards, fests and cook-offs have been named for Goodnight (far left) and Loving (left).

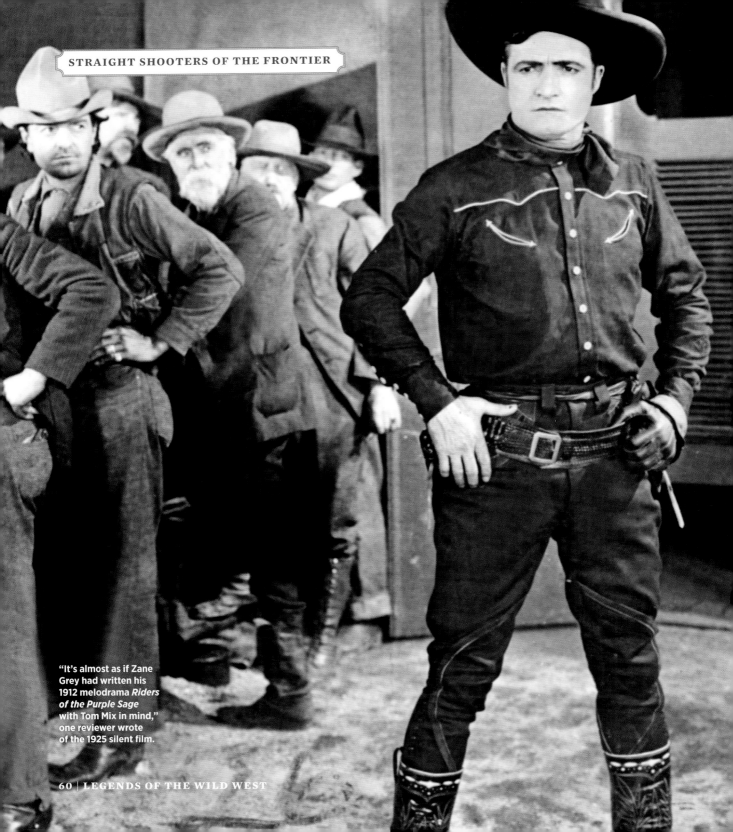

"It's almost as if Zane Grey had written his 1912 melodrama *Riders of the Purple Sage* with Tom Mix in mind," one reviewer wrote of the 1925 silent film.

THE LONG RIDERS

FROM MIX TO WAYNE TO EASTWOOD, AMERICA'S LOVE FOR THE WEST HAS BEEN SHAPED—AND RESHAPED—BY HOLLYWOOD. HERE ARE THE 10 BIGGEST PLAINS PLAYERS.

TOM MIX

HIS REEL REP Hollywood's first true Western legend, he brought glitz and glamour to the rough-and-tumble genre's silent era. He looked good, dressed sharp and made films full of spectacles and stunts—many of which he did on his own, causing career-long ailments. Born in 1880 and taught to ride by his stable-master dad, Mix enlisted to fight in the Spanish-American War but then ran off to get married. At the height of his fame in the 1920s, he built a 12-acre set called Mixville, which included a completely realistic re-creation of a frontier town. He also had a fan club with membership numbering about 2 million, and two well-trained horses named Tony and Tony Jr., who were favorites among fans. Mix died in a car accident at age 60.

BIG BREAK After showcasing his cattleman skills in the documentary short *Ranch Life in the Great Southwest* in 1909, his star rose, and he made 100 shorts through the next decade.

WORDS TO LIVE BY "The Old West is not a certain place in a certain time; it's a state of mind. It's whatever you want it to be."

POPULAR SCREEN PARDNERS Fellow actor/director Leo Maloney; leading lady Victoria Forde, whom Mix married in 1918.

FIVE ESSENTIALS TO VIEW The 1909 silent short *The Cowboy Millionaire* marked his Western debut; *Riders of the Purple Sage* (1925), based on the classic by Zane Grey; 1926's *The Great K & A Train Robbery*, based on the real-life foiling of a rail heist; the first of his talkies, 1932's *Destry Rides Again*; and his last role, as a Texas Ranger out to avenge the murder of his father in the 15-episode serial *The Miracle Rider* (1935).

FUN-TIER FACTS Mix was a pallbearer at his pal Wyatt Earp's funeral in 1929; his face is visible on the cover of the Beatles' *Sgt. Pepper's Lonely Hearts Club Band*.

RIDING HIGH
At the peak of his career, Tom Mix was the highest-paid actor in Hollywood, earning an average of $17,500 a week (about $218,000 in today's money).

JOHN WAYNE

HIS REEL REP No performer will ever be more associated with the Western than the Duke, who spent decades playing the definitive stalwart and sturdy Plains hero. His deliberate gait and way of speaking grew to be much-loved mannerisms that propelled him to a level of stardom few stars would ever approach. Born in 1907, Wayne and his family moved several times, ending up in California. After an injury curtailed his college athletic career, Wayne joined the prop department at Fox Studio and was befriended by young director John Ford, with whom Wayne would eventually make 31 films. In those and many more of his 169 features, he defined the 10-gallon-hat-wearing man's man for millions. When Soviet leader Nikita Khrushchev visited the U.S. in 1959, his two requests were to visit Disneyland and meet John Wayne.

BIG BREAK His first starring role, 1930's *The Big Trail*, was a box-office flop. (It was released as a widescreen film at a time when most theaters didn't show them.) It would take another nine years of low-budget "B" movies for Wayne to finally break out, in John Ford's classic *Stagecoach*, playing the rifle-spinning, Injun-shooting, fallen-angel-loving Ringo Kid.

WORDS TO LIVE BY "All I do is sell sincerity and I've been selling the hell out of that since I started."

POPULAR SCREEN PARDNERS Frequent co-stars include Ward Bond (the pair made 23 films together), Walter Brennan and Maureen O'Hara.

FIVE ESSENTIALS TO VIEW Howard Hawks' 1948 cattle-run classic *Red River*, co-starring Montgomery Clift; John Ford's *The Searchers*

(1956), considered among the greatest films ever made; Hawks' utterly winning *Rio Bravo* (1956), with Wayne's Texas sheriff and his allies helping keep a town safe from one bad local rancher; Wayne's Oscar-winning turn as Rooster Cogburn in 1969's *True Grit*; and his swan song, playing the go-out-gunning J.B. Books in *The Shootist* (1976).

FUN-TIER FACTS Wayne nearly starred in 1966's *The Dirty Dozen* (the role ultimately went to Lee Marvin), and had hoped to play the title role in 1971's *Dirty Harry* before it went to Clint Eastwood; he was, in the early 1930s, one of the first "Singing Cowboys" of the era—his voice, however, was dubbed for that of an off-screen performer.

WESTERN AVENGER
Randolph Scott fully embodied the haunted ex-sheriff who blames himself for his wife's death, and then hunts the men who killed her, in *7 Men From Now*.

RANDOLPH SCOTT

HIS REEL REP You can't find a star of the 1940s and '50s who made a greater contribution to the genre than Scott. Over half of the 100 films he made were Westerns. Like the best movie stars whose images evolve with age, he played roles that leaned heavily on his easygoing charm in the early part of his career, rode tall in the saddle as a fearless lawman in the middle, and ended his career as a grizzled symbol of the Old West.

BIG BREAK Word is that Scott, while doing bit parts after coming to Hollywood in 1927, was a dialect coach for Gary Cooper during production of *The Virginian* (1929), which was directed by Victor Fleming. It would be seven more years of "B" Westerns and other films before the 1936 adaptation of James Fenimore Cooper's *The Last of the Mohicans* turned Scott into a bona fide star.

WORDS TO LIVE BY "Westerns are a type of picture which everybody can see and enjoy. Westerns always make money. And they always increase a star's fan following."

POPULAR SCREEN PARDNERS Director Henry Hathaway; co-star Gabby Hayes; director Budd Boetticher.

FIVE ESSENTIALS TO VIEW Scott's first real starring role came in the 1932 rancher versus outlaw Western *Heritage of the Desert*, one of several films he'd make based on the works of Zane Grey; *Abilene Town*, the 1946 film that established him as a Western star in the minds of film fans; *7 Men From Now* (1956), the first of his seven films with Boetticher, and a role that John Wayne suggested he play; his next Boetticher collaboration, 1957's *The Tall T*, based on an Elmore Leonard story; and his final film, 1962's *Ride the High Country*, a critically acclaimed classic from director Sam Peckinpah about the Western outsider outliving his time on the Plains but keeping to his code.

FUN-TIER FACTS The intensely private Scott shared a beach house in Malibu with fellow star Cary Grant for 12 years, causing speculation about his sexuality (his 1944 marriage lasted 43 years, until his death in 1987); he was also name-checked in both the film *Blazing Saddles* and the Tom Lehrer song "Send the Marines."

JAMES STEWART

HIS REEL REP The beloved everyman with a deep moral code and distinctive drawl thrilled Western fans with unrelenting charm one minute, complicated goals the next and a strong pursuit of justice always. The World War II Army Air Force hero (he rose from private to colonel during the war) was a success in all film genres; like Gary Cooper, he made a series of Westerns that helped maintain his fame.

BIG BREAK In 1939—long considered Hollywood's greatest year—Stewart took his place as a top-draw star with *Mr. Smith Goes to Washington*, which was followed by his winning and winking Western parody *Destry Rides Again*, opposite actress Marlene Dietrich.

WORDS TO LIVE BY "I have my own rules and adhere to them. The rule is simple but inflexible. A James Stewart picture must have two vital ingredients: It will be clean and it will involve the triumph of the underdog over the bully."

POPULAR SCREEN PARDNERS Directors Alfred Hitchcock, Frank Capra and Anthony Mann; co-stars Henry Fonda, Lionel Barrymore and Margaret Sullavan.

FIVE ESSENTIALS TO VIEW *Bend of the River* (1952) found Stewart fronting a psychological thriller as a man prepared to do anything to safely lead a wagon train away from danger; the next year, he and director Anthony Mann got even darker, with Stewart pushing the boundaries of what it means to get justice in 1953's *The Naked Spur*; John Ford's 1962 "print the legend" classic *The Man Who Shot Liberty Valance*, with Stewart as Ransom Stoddard, the moral conscience alongside John

Wayne's torn and untamed rancher; that same year, Stewart took part in *How the West Was Won*, a family saga covering the decades-long movement West; and best pals Stewart and Henry Fonda chewed the scenery beautifully in *The Cheyenne Social Club* (1970) with both shining as aging cowboys who discover that one—Stewart's character—has inherited a brothel.

FUN-TIER FACTS Stewart's first film after returning from World War II action, *It's a Wonderful Life*, didn't become a success until decades after its release; he is one of the rare actors to win an Oscar for a comedy: *The Philadelphia Story* (1940).

LEADING MAN
Films such as *Bend of the River* and his Hitchcock collaborations introduced viewers to an edgier kind of Stewart persona during the 1950s that widened his star appeal.

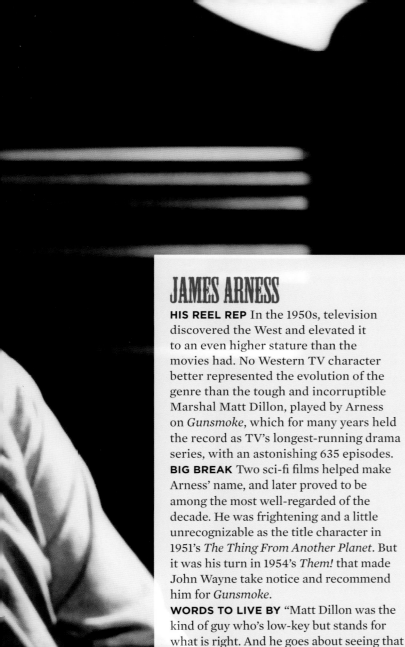

JAMES ARNESS

HIS REEL REP In the 1950s, television discovered the West and elevated it to an even higher stature than the movies had. No Western TV character better represented the evolution of the genre than the tough and incorruptible Marshal Matt Dillon, played by Arness on *Gunsmoke,* which for many years held the record as TV's longest-running drama series, with an astonishing 635 episodes.

BIG BREAK Two sci-fi films helped make Arness' name, and later proved to be among the most well-regarded of the decade. He was frightening and a little unrecognizable as the title character in 1951's *The Thing From Another Planet.* But it was his turn in 1954's *Them!* that made John Wayne take notice and recommend him for *Gunsmoke.*

WORDS TO LIVE BY "Matt Dillon was the kind of guy who's low-key but stands for what is right. And he goes about seeing that things turn out that way—with, of course, a lot of people suffering along the way."

POPULAR SCREEN PARDNERS Co-stars John Wayne, Milburn Stone, Amanda Blake, Ken Curtis and Dennis Weaver.

FIVE ESSENTIALS TO VIEW In 1953's *Hondo,* Arness plays a scout opposite Wayne's outlaw with a past who tries to help New Mexico homesteaders; starting in 1955, Arness began his 20-year run playing the Wyatt Earp–like Matt Dillon on *Gunsmoke,* patrolling Dodge City, Kansas, with Miss Kitty, Doc and Chester by his side; in *Gun the Man Down* (1956), he's an outlaw who, after being framed by his heist partners, gets out of jail and seeks revenge; the 1977–1979 TV series *How the West Was Won* kept Arness' profile high (and made him an international star), playing mountain man and family patriarch Zeb Macahan; and 12 years after he hung up Dillon's 10-gallon hat, Arness came home to the role that made him famous in the first of a series of TV movies: 1987's *Gunsmoke: Return to Dodge.* It features the now-former marshal back in Dodge after being injured, only to find himself going toe to toe with an old foe. Four more *Gunsmoke* movies would be filmed, with the final one released in 1993.

FUN-TIER FACTS Arness' brother was *Mission: Impossible* star Peter Graves; in one stretch, *Gunsmoke* was television's top-rated show for four years straight.

GARY COOPER

HIS REEL REP The sense of authenticity and heroism he brought to films throughout his career lent great emotional weight to his performances in Westerns. After establishing his name with a Western in 1929, his returns to the genre were celebrated, when he wasn't busy making the likes of *Mr. Deeds Goes to Town*, *Sergeant York*, *The Lives of a Bengal Lancer*, *For Whom the Bell Tolls* and *The Fountainhead*. And many consider *High Noon* to be among his—and the genre's—best ever.

BIG BREAK If Cooper really did call *The Virginian* the favorite of his films, there would be good reason for it. The 1929 early talkie based on Owen Wister's classic tale cast Cooper as the definitive strong-and-silent mysterious stranger who woos a schoolmarm and keeps to his principles. It established him as a major star.

WORDS TO LIVE BY "Naturalness is hard to talk about, but I guess it boils down to this: You find out what people expect of your type of character and then you give them what they want. That way, an actor never seems unnatural or affected no matter what role he plays."

POPULAR SCREEN PARDNERS Co-star Walter Brennan (they made 10 films together); director Henry Hathaway.

FIVE ESSENTIALS TO VIEW The sprawling, popular 1936 Cecil B. DeMille epic *The Plainsman*, in which Cooper plays a highly fictionalized version of Wild Bill Hickok; *The Westerner* (1940), with Cooper as the drifter cowboy who beats hanging judge Roy Bean at his own game; *High Noon* (1952), Hollywood's greatest "one man makes all the difference" film, with Cooper's Oscar-winning turn as marshal Will Kane taking on the bad guys (and, metaphorically, the House Un-American Activities Committee); playing a gentle Quaker who searches for redemption in the 1957 Civil War drama *Friendly Persuasion*; and *Man of the West* (1958), with Cooper's reformed outlaw struggling with the demons of his past that come back to haunt him when he confronts his former gang.

FUN-TIER FACTS His 20-year friendship with Ernest Hemingway began after the Nobel Prize–winning author based his main character in *For Whom the Bell Tolls* on Cooper; he maintained a lifelong love of Western history.

CLASSIC HERO
Gary Cooper, who had issues with back pain and had recently undergone surgery for a bleeding ulcer, wore no makeup and did his own stunt scenes, which made his *High Noon* character's pain much more evident.

HENRY FONDA

HIS REEL REP Much like contemporaries James Stewart and Gary Cooper, he wore the cloak of sincerity through a great many film genres; when he sported it while also wearing a 10-gallon hat, it took on deeper resonance. And yet, there may be no more winning shift from hero to villain than when he reluctantly chose to play the blue-eyed heavy in one of the most famous Spaghetti Westerns of all time.

BIG BREAK Fonda traded a nice career on Broadway for the lure of Hollywood, and while he shone in early films such as *Jezebel* and *Young Mr. Lincoln*, there was no looking back after he played Tom Joad in *The Grapes of Wrath*, a truly iconic role that landed at No. 12 on the American Film Institute's list of greatest film heroes.

WORDS TO LIVE BY "I am not a very interesting person. I haven't ever done anything except be other people. I ain't really Henry Fonda! Nobody could be. Nobody could have that much integrity."

POPULAR SCREEN PARDNERS Director John Ford; co-star Jane Darwell.

FIVE ESSENTIALS TO VIEW What 1939's *Jesse James* perhaps loses in historical accuracy it makes up for in power and popularity, with a young Fonda as Frank James opposite Tyrone Power; *The Ox-Bow Incident* (1943) sees Fonda fronting a tale of mob mentality, injustice and remorse; in John Ford's *My Darling Clementine* (1946), Fonda and Victor Mature co-star in what many regard as the screen's most satisfying telling of the Gunfight at the O.K. Corral; in 1948, Fonda co-starred with John Wayne in *Fort Apache*, playing an inflexible lieutenant colonel whose actions put the lives of his

men in danger; and when Fonda played the sadistic, remorseless psychopath Frank in *Once Upon a Time in the West*, Sergio Leone's 1968 Spaghetti Western, it proved that he could pretty much do anything.

FUN-TIER FACTS Fonda became the oldest man (76) to win a Best Actor Oscar when he took home the award opposite Katharine Hepburn in 1981's *On Golden Pond*; Sergio Leone only accepted Hollywood's offer to make *Once Upon a Time in the West* when Paramount Pictures told him he could potentially cast his favorite-ever actor: Fonda.

RUTHLESS STARE
Henry Fonda originally wanted to wear brown contact lenses to hide his natural color in *Once Upon a Time in the West*, but Sergio Leone insisted his icy blue eyes were right for the cold-blooded killer Frank.

CLINT EASTWOOD

HIS REEL REP When the Eisenhower-era 1950s turned to the counterculture 1960s, John Wayne's frontier hero was replaced by the ultimate Western anti-hero: Clint Eastwood's *Man With No Name*, who rode into town with a cheroot in his teeth, a poncho around his shoulders and, when pushed, murder on his mind. He would become the genre's top film star for decades.

BIG BREAK Eastwood found little success until he was tapped to play Rowdy Yates in TV's *Rawhide*, about the challenges of a cattle drive. Toward the end of the series, he was cast by little-known Italian director Sergio Leone to star in *A Fistful of Dollars*.

WORDS TO LIVE BY "I wanted to play [the Man With No Name] with an economy of words and create this whole feeling through attitude and movement. It was just the kind of character I had envisioned for a long time, keep to the mystery and allude to what happened in the past. I felt the less he said, the stronger he became."

POPULAR SCREEN PARDNERS Co-stars Morgan Freeman and ex-partner Sondra Locke; director Sergio Leone.

FIVE ESSENTIALS TO VIEW *The Good, the Bad and the Ugly* (1966) concludes Leone's incomparable Dollars Trilogy, with Eastwood cast as the "good" opposite the "bad" Lee Van Cleef and the "ugly" Eli Wallach; as "The Stranger" in 1972's *High Plains Drifter*, Eastwood rides into a corrupt mining town, metes out frontier justice and leaves in a cloud of dust; four years later, he directed and starred in *The Outlaw Josey Wales* as a Missouri man who seeks revenge after the post-Civil War murder of his family; in 1985, Eastwood took on the ghostly "Preacher," who intervenes in favor of a prospecting village being bullied by a mining company in *Pale Rider*; and Eastwood directed, produced and starred in the 1992 Oscar-winning best picture *Unforgiven*, as Will Munny, a onetime outlaw who struggles with his past as he heads into a Wyoming town to right an ugly wrong.

FUN-TIER FACTS In 1986, Eastwood was elected mayor of his town of Carmel-by-the-Sea, California; a noted composer, he has also scored several of his films, including the box-office hits *Million Dollar Baby* and *Mystic River*.

JAMES GARNER

HIS REEL REP Wait, Westerns...could be funny? Definitely if the right star was marshaling the mirth. Enter Garner's Bret Maverick, an Old West poker king who was an ace at getting into and out of trouble. The role perfectly suited Garner's subtlety and sensibility, which he then brought to a wide range of television and film roles in a career that touched upon Westerns throughout the years.

FAMILY AFFAIR The usual format for *Maverick* had Garner's Bret Maverick switching off in each episode with his brother Bart (Jack Kelly), although they sometimes appeared together (and Garner once played their dad, Beau "Pappy" Maverick).

BIG BREAK Garner had nearly gotten the title role in television's first-ever hourlong drama, the Western series *Cheyenne*, but instead ended up guesting on four episodes; he also lobbied for and won a part in the Marlon Brando drama *Sayonara*. These led him to his star turn as television's *Maverick*.

WORDS TO LIVE BY "The characters I've played, especially Bret Maverick and Jim Rockford [in *The Rockford Files*], almost never use a gun, and they always try to use their wits instead of their fists."

POPULAR SCREEN PARDNERS Co-stars Jack Kelly, Noah Beery and Julie Andrews.

FIVE ESSENTIALS TO VIEW 1957's *Maverick*, with Garner as one half of a set of Texas poker-player brothers, who roam from town to town, humorously working through life-or-death situations in the Old West; in 1966's *Duel at Diablo*, Garner is out to find the murderer of his Comanche wife in a film about complicated relations with the Indians that marked Sidney Poitier's Western debut; *Hour of the Gun* (1967) finds Garner playing Wyatt Earp in director Preston Sturges' more factual account of the Gunfight at the O.K. Corral; in 1969, Garner returned to that familiar line between wit and the West in *Support Your Local Sheriff!* about a gunfighter passing through town who ends up setting a spell; and *Streets of Laredo*, the 1995 sequel to *Lonesome Dove*, which stars Garner as Woodrow Call, who's hunting a notorious killer who is hardly older than a boy.

FUN-TIER FACTS He won an Emmy for playing Jim Rockford in *The Rockford Files*, and was nominated for a Best Actor Oscar for *Murphy's Romance*; his chemistry with Mariette Hartley in a series of Polaroid commercials had viewers believing the two were actually married.

ROBERT DUVALL

HIS REEL REP *The Godfather*. *The Great Santini*. *Network*. *The Apostle*. Duvall's credits speak to the depth of his "actor's actor" career. And like some of the best classic Hollywood stars on this list from past decades, Duvall has brought that same never-say-die toughness to a ton of Western performances that loom large today.

BIG BREAK After a wealth of appearances on Broadway and in TV dramas, Duvall made a memorable film debut, showing up at the end of 1962's *To Kill a Mockingbird* as the reclusive and ultimately heroic Boo Radley. He got the part on the recommendation of screenwriter Horton Foote, who would later script Duvall's Oscar-winning role in *Tender Mercies*.

WORDS TO LIVE BY "Spending two years on my uncle's ranch in Montana as a young man gave me the wisdom and the thrust to do Westerns."

POPULAR SCREEN PARDNERS Director Francis Ford Coppola; co-stars Tommy Lee Jones, James Caan and Laurence Olivier.

FIVE ESSENTIALS TO VIEW We don't see a great deal of him in 1970's *True Grit*, but we wait all film long to see John Wayne confront Duvall's evil outlaw "Lucky" Ned Pepper, and it's worth it; in 1983, Duvall won an Oscar playing Mac Sledge, an alcoholic country singer redeemed by love in the modern Western *Tender Mercies*; in 1989's epic miniseries *Lonesome Dove*, he is Gus McCrae opposite Tommy Lee Jones' Woodrow Call, two former Texas Rangers who embark on the ultimate cattle-driving adventure and a whole lot more; in 2003's *Open Range*, Duvall and Kevin Costner are cattlemen driving a herd across the country who must deal with a ruthless land baron; and Duvall won an Emmy for his lead performance in the 2006 Western miniseries *Broken Trail*, as an aging cowboy transporting horses from Oregon to Wyoming in 1898 whose journey is interrupted when he tries to rescue five Chinese girls from a life of prostitution.

FUN-TIER FACTS Duvall is a skilled Argentine tango dancer who owns two dance studios; for his performance in *Tender Mercies*, Duvall had it added into his contract that he'd be allowed to sing the songs his character performs in the film. ★

LIVING THE LIFE
"The English have Shakespeare, the French have Molière, the Russians have Chekhov. The Western is ours," Duvall once said. Today, the actor lives on a 360-acre horse farm in northern Virginia.

More than 300,000 people headed to California to try their luck panning for gold.

CHAPTER THREE

RUSHES, RUNS AND RAILROADS

The promise of
"striking it rich"
brought panhandlers
by the thousands
to California.

GOLDEN YEARS

WHAT A RUSH! WHEN A CRY OF "GOLD!" CAME UP, SCORES OF FOLKS HEADED FOR CALIFORNIA, CHANGING THE WEST FOREVER.

non–Native Americans living in California when carpenter John Marshall found ore as he helped build Sutter's Mill in 1848. In the months after Marshall's find, the nonindigenous population soared to 300,000.

✪ It didn't pay to be first: Marshall died penniless in 1885. His boss, Swiss immigrant Johann Sutter, didn't fare much better. Sutter's property (near Sacramento) was overtaken and destroyed by prospectors, and he tried for years to get Congress to reimburse him. He died in 1880, a bitter man.

✪ Prospectors mined some 12 million ounces of the shiny stuff during the heat of the Gold Rush—by today's numbers, that's $20 billion worth—but that includes only what was reported. The hushed-up profits likely doubled that. In fact, the California bounty was so bodacious that the territory was fast-tracked to statehood in just over a year.

✪ The vast majority of the prospectors (aka "forty-niners") were Americans, but the lure of gold also drew immigrants from Europe, Australia, Latin America and Asia. More than 25,000 miners came from China.

TOUGH LUCK
Unfortunate futures met carpenter John Marshall (top left) and his boss, Johann Sutter (top right), but Marshall's first find started a golden migration.

AT THE CENTER
Sutter's Mill (above) became gold rush's ground zero, but before Sutter could profit, eager prospectors overran the place in their quest for ore.

EVERYONE KNOWS ABOUT THE Gold Rush of 1849: A nugget of ore is discovered in California. Word spreads like wildfire. Fortune hunters flock west. Some get rich. Some don't. And that's it, right? Oh, hell no! Here are 22 startling truths about an event that shook the nation like no other.

✪ The search for gold in California resulted in the largest mass migration in United States history. There were barely 800

✪ Karl Marx, founder of Communism, claimed the Gold Rush shifted his views on political economy, serving as an inspiration for his 1867 manifesto, *Das Kapital*.

✪ Few solo prospectors struck pay dirt, because mining was a corporate game. "A prospector might draw attention to the existence of ore, but it took a sizable investment to get it [via hydraulic mining]," says history professor John Findlay. "Only big companies had the resources to do that." Flash forward 170 years: Not much has changed in America.

✪ California's first psychiatric institution—Stockton State Hospital—opened its doors in 1851 to accommodate the legions of prospectors suffering from mental health disorders brought on by gold fever.

✪ "The image of the grizzled old prospector with the burro, moseying along and making a fortune persisted—and for good reason," notes American West authority Patty Limerick. "It's an attractive counterpoint [to the truth]." And how: Violence was the order of the day, with immigrant settlers and indigenous peoples the frequent victims.

✪ By 1850, only 3 percent of those who'd come for the Rush were women. Male prostitution and female impersonation flourished. San Francisco was the "City of Bachelors."

✪ Not everyone hoped to become a zillionaire. "Ambitions were modest," says Stanford University historian Richard White. "Most men wanted to make enough to return to the East and establish a store or buy a farm. The miners who remained didn't

"Your streams have minnows and ours are paved with gold."

Letter published in the Philadelphia newspaper North American *in September 1949*

———◆◆◆◆———

do it because they were a great success. It was because they were failures."

✪ Who hit the single biggest jackpot? Trader John Murphy reportedly gave a blanket to a Native American in exchange for a gold nugget valued at $130,000 in today's money.

✪ Some discoveries happened by accident. A *New York Times* write-up from the era claims an Alpine County, California, woman found a chunk of gold—today worth more than $46,000—while playing fetch with her dog. Another report said a nugget worth $559,000 was dug by a miner as he prepared a grave for a drowned companion.

✪ British prospector Edward Hargraves failed miserably as a forty-niner, then left for New South Wales. After he arrived, he happened upon five specks of gold in a creek and launched the 1851 Australian Gold Rush.

✪ Prices were insane! A hotel room in San Francisco could run you $10,000 per month (that's $300,000 today). And don't expect free breakfast: A meal of bread, cheese,

sardines and beer would cost an additional $43. A dish called the Hangtown Fry—an omelet dripping in bacon fat topped with fried oysters—was the menu's priciest item.

✪ The businessmen who sold much-needed products pocketed way more dough than the miners: Sturdy boots ran $3,000. One of the best-known entrepreneurs, Levi Strauss, hit San Francisco in 1850 with plans to manufacture heavy-duty canvas tents and wagon covers. But he realized there was a greater need for his industrial-strength denim—so he wound up making pants.

✪ Strauss wasn't the only future super-mogul in gold country. Philip Armour, who'd later establish the Chicago-based meat business Armour & Company, started his fortune in California by constructing the sluices that controlled river flow. John Studebaker, who manufactured wheelbarrows for the miners, went on to make Civil War–era wagons. That thriving enterprise would one day become the Studebaker automobile company. Wells Fargo & Company started its banking services as a safe way to ship gold back East.

✪ The Golden Gate Bridge had nothing to do with the Gold Rush. The strait the bridge now spans was named Golden Gate two years before gold was discovered—because it provided a golden passage to the Orient.

✪ California's Death Valley (known to hit 134°F, the hottest temperature on Earth) got its notorious name in just the way you'd assume: In 1849, 13 prospectors died while trying to traverse the region on their way to gold country.

✪ Abandon ship! The chance for wealth was so seductive, many sailors fled vessels upon docking in San Francisco and joined the treasure hunt. Without crews to man return trips, many ships were converted into warehouses, saloons and hotels, even jails. Others were dismantled and used for building supplies. At least a dozen remain at the bottom of San Francisco Bay.

✪ Horror maestro Edgar Allan Poe was so annoyed by all the Gold Rush fuss that he created a hoax to discourage wannabe prospectors. His newspaper article "Von Kempelen and his Discovery"—published in a Boston weekly—claimed that a German scientist had figured out a way to turn lead into gold. Few fell for it.

✪ San Francisco still boomed in the post–Gold Rush years, but entertainment remained so scarce that two stray dogs, Bummer and Lazarus, became celebrities. The pups not only charmed the locals but were also expert rat catchers—at one point terminating 85 varmints in 20 minutes. Upon their deaths, they were stuffed and mounted for public viewing, with both earning gushing newspaper obits. Bummer's was written by Mark Twain.

✪ Truth be told, what went down in California wasn't America's first Gold Rush. That actually occurred 50 years earlier, when a 17-pound nugget was found in Cabarrus County, North Carolina. Some 30,000 fortune hunters swarmed to the state. The haul was so big that for the next 30 years, every U.S.-minted gold coin was made using Tar Heel gold. ★

LASTING LEGACIES
Bannack, Montana, drew hopeful prospectors in 1862 after gold was discovered in Grasshopper Creek. The Bannack State Park (opposite page, top) is open to visitors with over 60 historic mining town structures to explore. The Goldfield Ghost Town in Apache Junction, Arizona (opposite page, bottom right), is home to the Mammoth Gold Mine. Visitors can walk down the historic streets of the town that flourished in the 1890s. Levi Strauss made a fortune selling his sturdy denim pants (above) to miners.

Out on the range, a gun, a lasso and a saddle were essentials for helping a cowboy do his job.

TOOLS OF THE TRADE

IN THE WEST, GUNMEN, COWBOYS AND HOMESTEADERS HAD ONE BIG THING IN COMMON: THE NEED FOR THE RIGHT GEAR TO SURVIVE.

CREATURE COMFORTS
A cast-iron stove like the one shown here (above) was based in part on the "Pennsylvania Fireplace," invented by Benjamin Franklin in 1740, and used for both cooking and heat. The classic deep-bed covered wagon (left) was originally made in Pennsylvania's Conestoga River valley.

WHAT DO YOU DO IF YOUR job title is "mountain man," and you roam the West in search of beaver pelts to sell for a living? If you're famed scout Kit Carson (inset below), you carry your world with you. After all, a good coat (Carson's was made of deer skins he left out to harden, for better protection) and the right horse (his was named Apache) will only get you so far, especially if arrows or bear claws might be in your future.

Many states printed guidebooks detailing tools for travelers to bring to the West, and each profession required its own specialty technology. Barbed wire, patented in the mid-1870s and perfect for penning in cattle, "became ubiquitous" for homesteaders, says professor Durwood Ball from the University of New Mexico.

With money tight, you always wanted to make the most of what you had. Here are the top items that different groups of Westerners needed for survival.

On the Farm

PASSAGE OUT WEST Of course, you can't get to your new plot of land without the most famed vehicle in the plains, the horse-drawn covered wagon. Their wheel bearings fashioned from iron and wood, the canvas-covered Conestoga wagons kept your load—drawn by your horses, mules or oxen and totaling as much as 6 tons of goods and people—as steady as possible over rough

terrain. And consider that your belongings (furniture, cooking equipment, clothing) would be greater than what would fit these days in the typical moving van. It also helped to have an expert in wagon maintenance among your party, given that the poor roads and unpredictability of weather, from rains to bad dry spells, could wreak havoc on your wheels, which needed constant greasing.

A WAY TO BUILD You've gotten to your destination...now what? If you're putting down stakes, you want to move from the wagon into a home (as the Homestead Act demanded). If there's wood around (no guarantee), your construction issues are easier. Otherwise, many homesteaders used masses of tightly rooted grass and sod that were cut into bricks and stacked. More grass and sod went atop whatever long poles you

found for rafters, and ditches dug around the property helped ensure that your house wouldn't wash away in a flooding rain. Your floor was the dirt you built upon.

THE PUMP THAT CATCHES THE WIND Since there was no living without water, a well had to be dug—which was its own issue, requiring the correct drilling apparatus to go as deep as 300 feet. And once a well was dug, help was needed to pump water. With the West having wind in abundance, the American windmill, first developed in 1854, became a plains staple—more than 1 million were in use. Initially made of wood, metal models later became more common. The wood version could be creaky and required maintenance, but all that mattered was the angle: It had to be poised so that the wind would pump the water to the most efficient degree.

HOME SWEET HOME
Bricks of sod, an iron turbine windmill and hired hands were the homesteader's path to making it out West.

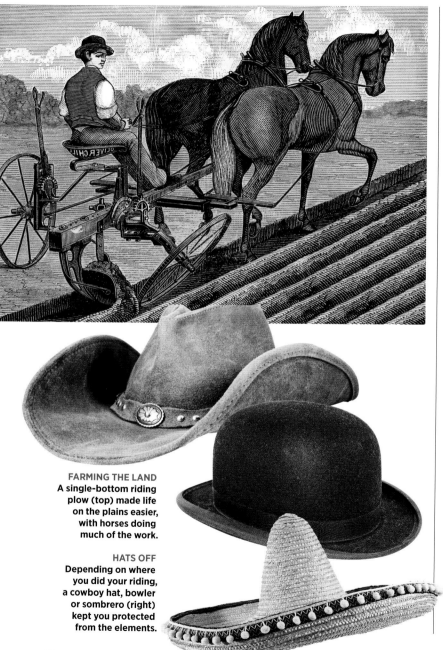

NOW YOU'RE COOKING The Dutch oven, the official state cooking pot of Texas, Utah and Arkansas, was a "critical thing for any family moving West," says Ball. Dutch ovens were so valuable that they were passed down through generations, and the cast-iron, thick-walled pots were de rigueur for making the cross-country passage. Otherwise, the more traditional cast-iron stoves or fireplaces were used for cooking, with wood, corncobs or dried animal dung being used for fuel. Regulating temperature required great precision.

GOING DEEP Granted, you weren't getting new clothes without a spinning wheel to make wool into thread, but a farmer wasn't getting anywhere without the right handheld tools, either. Those included a reaper to separate grain from chaff and a scythe to cut across the land. The commercial steel plow, invented by John Deere in 1837, helped farmers go deeper into the tough prairie soil. The innovative, curved blade design, combined with a steel-blade construction that cut better through stickier dirt, gave the farmer a fighting chance for profits.

On the Cow Ranch

HEADGEAR John Wayne rode from out in the distance with his trusty 10-gallon perched on his brow, and that celebrates the exceedingly popular wares of the John B. Stetson Company, founded in 1865. Prior to that, hat styles were often regional. In Texas, cowhands usually wore flat-crowned felt hats that were more popular among the Pueblo in Mexico. Sombreros were also common. A bowler-style hat was also prevalent for a time. Beyond region, it was a question of making sure your hat stayed on when the winds were strong. Thus, the

FARMING THE LAND
A single-bottom riding plow (top) made life on the plains easier, with horses doing much of the work.

HATS OFF
Depending on where you did your riding, a cowboy hat, bowler or sombrero (right) kept you protected from the elements.

addition of "bonnet strings" to tie a hat down and a band around the brim to keep the fit tight, plus the necessary bandanna, which acted as a combo dirt filter, washcloth and, when necessary, sling.

A CUT ABOVE Few things came in handier for a cowhand than a reliable fixed-blade sheath knife. With its 6- to 8-inch blade, the same tool could be called upon to split firewood, clean game or hunt, as necessary, before being sharpened when the right stone presented itself. True, its utilitarian purpose sometimes gave way to self-defense, often with a longer blade. The famed Bowie knife, with its more ornate, swordlike, hand-protecting cross guard, worked well when things got out of hand.

RUMBLE SEAT When the song refers to the "Home on the Range," that home was often the most important cowhand accessory there was: the right saddle. The Western stock version, designed after those used by Mexican cowboys (*vaqueros*) would begin with the "tree," aka the wood frame, covered by the softest rawhide leather available stretched atop it; it weighed, in total, about 40 pounds. It was wide and comfortable, with a slot for ventilation, a high cantle for good back support and stirrups deep enough to allow one to ride with their feet pushed forward for greater comfort and better weapon access. The steel horn could tow a cow or unearth a stuck wagon. A skirt behind the saddle seat held a blanket, and saddle strings tied down items such as a lariat or a rain jacket.

SEEING THE LIGHT John Wayne was always rolling cigarettes in the movies, lighting them with wooden matches he'd strike against anything. But until those matches became commonplace, a cowhand would use a tinderbox, a waterproof metal box filled with cotton or linen tinder and a suitable flint. A spark with a knife gets a flame going in the box, and closing the box puts it out. Tinder was replaceable, and you didn't have to worry about the apparatus getting wet. Also, everybody carried tobacco, whether they smoked or not: It was good to trade for something more useful.

FEET FIRST Chaps were a vital safeguard against anything harmful, from thorns to snakebites, as you rode through the thicket.

CLASSIC RIFLE
The Winchester 1873 (above), with its quick lever action, was favored by soldiers and hunters.

ALONG FOR THE RIDE
The Western stock saddle (below) was a cowhand's bench during the day (with a sheath knife the tool of choice) and pillow at night, with a bedroll strapped tightly through days of riding.

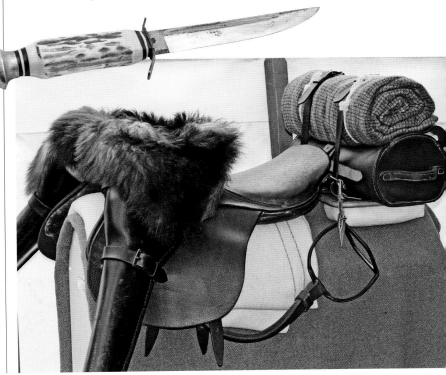

HOME ON THE RANGE
A cup and a canteen, a fire and some coffee were the cowhand necessities.

Plus, an extra layer on your legs, given all the saddle time, never hurt. Cowhands wore leather chaps over their jeans—courtesy of the Levi Strauss company, founded in 1853 in San Francisco—tucked into that most important item: their boots. These, by the way, were made of the best leather you could afford, rose above the calf, had thin soles to give you a "feel of the stirrup," 2-inch heels to keep them from slipping out of the ride, fancy stitching and hooks to pull them on—and they were tight enough in the leg that a U-shaped, heel-gripping boot jack was needed to remove them. The chaps were similar to the leggings favored by Native American tribesmen. Spurs, by the way, were sometimes ornamental and often blunted to keep them from hurting the horse.

On the Frontier

WEAPONS OF CHOICE For mountain men, danger lurked around every bit of brush. Beyond your well-worn knife, you needed a firearm that promised accuracy, a long range, power, ease of use and durability. That would be the most up-to-date plains rifle you could buy. The Hawken rifle that trappers Kit Carson and Jim Bridger used had a 400-yard range and weighed 10 to 15 pounds, depending on the model. It was later replaced by the Henry rifle, courtesy of Winchester, most notably the lever-action, 15-round-magazine 1873 Winchester, known as The Gun that Won the West. And though no shoot-out is necessary, another weapon with a claim on that title might be the Peacemaker, Colt's .45 caliber six-shooting handgun that enjoyed its own run on the frontier.

DRINK IT IN Western legend sees riders forging trails through long stretches of unknown territory. Water was essential for sustenance and, if needed, medicinal help, and you couldn't be without at least one canteen. Holding at least two quarts of water (larger than current-day models), canteens were most frequently made of leather or sometimes steel, with a cloth or hand-sewn fabric cover that, when soaked in water, could cool the contents.

FLAVOR MAKERS The clichés about the culinary delights of the frontier are pretty accurate. When you were out on the range, bacon, biscuits (or hardtack) and beans might be in your future for a day's eats, but you also needed a few cooking supplies, usually consisting of a small pot, a tin plate, a mug and iron utensils. Your knife handled all the food prep (and, perhaps, brought in the game as well), and the one luxury brought along was a coffeepot.

LIVING BY WITS To say there were no creature comforts for the frontiersman is a vast understatement. So, in a sense, no "tool" was more important than ingenuity in the wild, both in terms of preparation and impulsive decision-making. A fishing line and hook came in handy when camp found you near water, with dug-up worms or grubs as bait. There were no doctors in the middle mountain ranges, so some kind of crude first-aid kit and a working knowledge of herbs and local plants was an absolute necessity, given that tending wounds and setting broken bones were frequent occurrences.

UNDER THE STARS The evolution of the sleeping bag has made camping in the elements a "roughing it" pleasure. The bedroll of the American West saw much cruder models. The aim was always the same: an item that was comfortable, protective and dry. Kit Carson and his fellow mountain men had to rely on something elementary—a dense, water-repellent woolen Mackinaw blanket, with a bearskin or buffalo robe on top for added warmth. Later, a wool blanket sandwiched between two rubber blankets served as the foundation, with a cowhand or soldier wrapped in that. It wasn't until the rubberized canvas-tarp bedroll gained greater use, later in the 19th century, that the plainsman could expect at least some guarantee not only of sleep comfort but of both an extra cushion to sit on and a place to store valuables once the bedroll was rolled back up and tied to the saddle. ★

QUICK ON THE DRAW
The Colt .45 evolved through years of manufacturing, with the single-action Army "Peacemaker" becoming the standard revolver.

HUMP DAYS
The Camel Experiment remains an odd, fascinating chapter of the West.

The brave soldier rides in from the distance and pulls in the reins on his trusty... camel? Seems odd, but for a time, just before the Civil War and then sporadically for about 50 years, the United States Camel Corps was a crew of 34 camels imported from Greece, Egypt and Turkey that were used as pack animals for long stretches in the desert and, later, for mining work. It's a sight that hardly relates to the image of noble steeds, but Richard White, a professor emeritus of American history at Stanford University, sees the logic.

"It was an experiment that failed—but it wasn't stupid," he says. "For much of the Southwest, you went a long way without water, and Army horses were not nearly as hearty and could not go nearly as far between water stops as Indian ponies could. The idea that you could get another animal that could keep on going was not a dumb one. But it never quite worked out. Handling them is very difficult, and none of the attempts got very far." But it would have made for a far different set of Western tales.

Theodore Judah's grand dream of a Central Pacific Railroad required the efforts of thousands of workers.

THE ROAD
THAT CHANGED
THE WEST

CONSTRUCTION WENT HAND IN HAND WITH
CORRUPTION—BUT IN THE END, THE
TRANSCONTINENTAL RAILROAD MADE
THE GROWTH OF THE COUNTRY POSSIBLE.

TOGETHER AT LAST
The Union Pacific
No. 119 met the
"Jupiter" Central
Pacific No. 60
at Promontory
Point, Utah, in the
ceremony to join
together the first
transcontinental
railroad. The effort
took six years and
stretched nearly
1,800 miles.

THE GUNS AND THE GOLD. THE trappers and troublemakers. The rustlers, rabble-rousers, con men and cowboys. The Wild West is filled with giant events, tales and characters. But none of them have the steam of the transcontinental railroad.

It would be difficult to find a single enterprise more important to the shaping of that part of the nation than the laying of wood, the driving of spikes and then, finally, the sound of trains rolling from the East to the West.

"The railroad, going from one coast to the other, accelerates development on the plains, changes the cattle industry and ties the country closer together," says University of Washington history professor John Findlay.

It's also the first time American ingenuity and its bitter twin brother, corruption, were practiced on so grand a scale. Let's track the crazy path it took to get it all together.

At first, it was all about trade. Asa Whitney, a dry-goods merchant who'd done business with China, was the first to see it: A railroad heading to the Pacific Coast would make travel (and, of course, trade) easier. The result would align the United States more profitably on the world stage, and Whitney petitioned Congress from the mid-1840s onward. In that time, peace with Mexico and the acquisition of California and Oregon made the plan sounder.

But nobody could agree on where it should go. Southerners in Congress argued against Whitney's idea, citing Indian interference. Also, the planned route was too far north to make it profitable for the South. An 1853 Pacific Railroad Survey Act led to a glorious 1,000-page study of the pluses and minuses of five different westbound routes— but, ridiculously, didn't pick a best one.

Then the Civil War changed everything. When the South seceded, the North-controlled Congress ran roughshod over policy, doing "more than any other [Congress] in history to change the course of national life," according to one historian. Among new laws: the 1862 Homestead Act (giving, essentially, free Western acreage to whoever claimed it), and the Pacific Railroad Act, which set the West-facing railroad build in motion. Central Pacific (building in the East)

and Union Pacific (building in the West) were to construct along the 42nd parallel, going through Chicago to the Oregon-California border. Congress granted aid for construction and about 150 million acres of land along the route to work with.

Big dreams had to be met by big bucks—and the Big Four. So named because of their size, not their wallets, the Big Four of Collis Huntington, Mark Hopkins, Leland Stanford and Charles Crocker had little in common, other than having come West to make it rich in the Gold Rush. Engineer and rail enthusiast Theodore Judah convinced them to sign on to the Central Pacific Railroad. They bought in, Judah died suddenly of yellow fever (a mosquito-borne disease) and they wound up running the Central Pacific—and realizing that the way to make it rich was through government construction subsidies. Thomas Durant ran Union Pacific, using a financial structure that would eventually land the company in a credit scandal.

Running things also included bringing in new workers. About 20,000 laborers contributed to the effort at all times. Irish workers made up the vast part of the Union Pacific. The Central Pacific eventually turned to Chinese immigrants and, finding their laboring extremely efficient, increased their numbers until, by 1867, they comprised as much as 90 percent of the force.

Then the two tracks met...and it was hard to "hammer out" an ending. The Union and Central tracks came together, ultimately, on May 10, 1869, in Promontory Point, Utah, and a giant ceremony celebrated the achievement. Chinese workers knocked in all but the final spike before being ushered out of the publicity picture. A golden spike (right) was there for the hitting: Leland

Stanford swung...and missed. Then it was Thomas Durant's turn to take a swing—he whiffed, too. Still, photos and the telegraph proclaimed the First Transcontinental Railroad open for business.

For Native Americans, the railroad spelled the true beginning of the end. The fumes of both construction and the trains themselves, filling once-clear skies, were a reminder that the railroad was the white man's way of asserting dominance over the land, treaties notwithstanding. Although many tribes visited violence upon construction teams, it was to no avail.

TOILING AWAY
Central Pacific Railroad supervisor Charles Crocker frequently broke daily construction records. Crews worked as many as 15 hours per day on the project.

Huntington

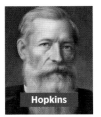

Hopkins

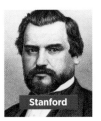

Stanford

Crocker

THE BIG FOUR
Collis Huntington, Mark Hopkins, Leland Stanford and Charles Crocker "were basically shopkeepers in Sacramento who put very little of their own money into the venture," says Professor Richard White—but they all made a handsome profit.

The railroad turned out to be "quantity over quality," with lots of greed and corruption thrown in. The tracks had been constructed quickly and hastily, with executives filling their pockets with monies they were allowed to charge farmers for land owned near the tracks. Also, more companies joined, building different lines of their own. "These railroads are going to be built very poorly, and they're going to go bankrupt repeatedly throughout the 19th century," says Stanford University professor emeritus Richard White. "As business enterprises, they don't work out, but as speculative enterprises, great fortunes [were] made."

Eventually, panic ensued. When financier Jay Cooke underestimated costs to build the Northern Pacific line westward and overestimated his ability to get more capital, the company went bankrupt, helping lead the U.S. into the Panic of 1873 and what was then called the Great Depression, with 55 railroad businesses failing and poor economic conditions lasting six years.

The moneymen finally found their footing again. Consolidation and regrouping followed, and the second transcontinental

The linking of the two rail lines in Promontory Point, Utah, led to one of the country's great photo opportunities ever.

line linked spikes in 1881. By 1893, that number would total five, as the country left its reliance on agriculture far behind, creating what professor Findlay calls "an industrial West that was integrated into the nation more than ever."

After that, it was all about growth—and a new way to travel. The railroad changed everything: Cattle were shipped by rail; the postal service carted letters and newspapers and magazines at full speed; the pace of life increased; and many more folks headed West. Through the haze of the engine smoke, there was no looking back for anybody. ★

DERAILED BY HOLLYWOOD

Train robberies in the Wild West became fodder for Hollywood adventure.

In famed photos, the ironically named Justus D. Barnes wore a period mustache and carried a loaded six-shooter. Yes, he came to Hollywood from Little Falls, New York, but he remains to this day a legend of the West, the vicious bandit in the first-ever movie blockbuster, 1903's *The Great Train Robbery*. At the end of the movie, in a moment that had nothing to do with the plot of the 12-minute film (and one that inspired the opening of every James Bond film since), Barnes raised his pistol and fired all six shots at the audience, with many people ducking to avoid the "realism" of the moment.

Barnes

Plenty of real train passengers were doing their own ducking not too many years prior, when robbers such as Butch Cassidy and the Sundance Kid and their famed gang took to the rail tracks to earn some riches. The robberies were events that inspired countless movie moments. Among the best:

- ✪ *JESSE JAMES* (1939)
- ✪ *WHISPERING SMITH* (1948)
- ✪ *SANTA FE* (1951)
- ✪ *THE PROFESSIONALS* (1966)
- ✪ *BUTCH CASSIDY AND THE SUNDANCE KID* (1969)
- ✪ *THE WILD BUNCH* (1969)
- ✪ *THE TRAIN ROBBERS* (1973)
- ✪ *THE LONG RIDERS* (1980)
- ✪ *THE GREY FOX* (1982)
- ✪ *FRANK AND JESSE* (1995)
- ✪ *THE LONE RANGER* (2013)

Butch (Paul Newman) and Sundance (Robert Redford), in one of 1969's best films.

Illustrator Edward Vebell captured the romantic spirit of cowboys guiding longhorns along the Chisholm Trail in the 1880s—along with the blissful disconnect between the myth and the reality.

THE
LONG
RUNS

THE CATTLE-TRAIL RIDES IN AMERICA LASTED
ONLY A SHORT TIME, BUT THE LEGENDS THEY
SPAWNED CREATED THE IMAGE OF THE COWBOY.

FREE TO ROAM
Cattle were permitted to spread out over several miles of terrain, making for treacherous going among the cowboys if the slightest unfamiliar sound set the animals to stampeding in all directions.

AMERICANS KNOW ALL ABOUT the cattle drives of the Old West because they saw Tom Dunston lead one of the most famous ones. In 1851, Dunston claimed a piece of land deep in southern Texas near the Rio Grande (shooting and killing a representative of the previous owner of the property to make his point before "reading over him" from his Bible) and, with one cow and a bull, set big dreams for the Red River D brand. "Give me 10 years, and I'll have that brand on the gates of the greatest ranch in Texas...on more cattle than you've looked at anywhere," he declared. "I'll have that brand on enough beef to feed the whole country. Good beef for hungry people. Beef to make 'em strong, make 'em grow. But it takes work, and it takes sweat, and it takes time, lots of time. It takes years."

It would, in fact, take 14 years before Dunston was ready to drive his 10,000 head of cattle the 1,000 miles to Missouri along the Chisholm Trail, and it did take work and sweat. That wasn't a real cattle drive, of course; it only felt like one because it was the one Dunston—played by John Wayne— led in 1948's *Red River*, a film that lets you in on some of the desperation and drama of the drive's true heyday, from the end of the Civil War to the mid-1880s. Those were the days when millions of longhorn cattle meandered along the path heading north, and the word "cowboy" began to take on a fresh new meaning.

Hollywood has had its way with the long cattle runs, perhaps most famously in the miniseries based on Larry McMurtry's novel *Lonesome Dove*. In the movies, the

drives—accompanied by a swirling musical soundtrack—are apt to depict a lonely and philosophical man on the range, but it would be difficult to convey the hoof-heavy danger and monotony inherent in a journey of over 1,000 miles, lasting three or four months, which involved riding as many as 14 hours per day.

"That was a very rough run," says Patty Limerick, PhD, faculty director and board chair of the Center of the American West at the University of Colorado Boulder. "In some cases, you're trying to get pretty wild longhorns to ford a river without dying."

But along with high-caliber events such as the Gunfight at the O.K. Corral, nothing propagated the legend of the West quite like the cattle runs, even if history didn't exactly match the myth in any of these categories.

The Clothes

The janglin' spurs. The 10-gallon hat. The accessories, like the twirlin', spinnin' lasso. In the movies, they make a cowboy look cool. In real life, they kept him from being killed. The chaps a cowboy wore over his denims weren't for show; they were there to keep thorns and other greenery from poking him along the way. The bandanna around his neck wasn't what we'd call a fashion statement; it was necessary to keep the sweat of exceedingly lengthy and hot days off his neck and brow and, when covering his nose and mouth—outlaw style—it kept the dust rustled up from the lines of cows and horses from choking him relentlessly as he rode. The higher heel of a cowboy boot decreased the chances that he'd be thrown from his horse when a sudden scare sent a line of cattle racing into the distance. The gun he carried? He actually fired it, when necessary, a whole lot more than he twirled it along his index finger. And while those roping tricks became, in the Buffalo Bill shows, the epitome of the rodeo-style art form, they were developed in part as a skill-based route to prevent getting your fingers cut off if a roped steer pulled too hard while your digits were pressed against a saddle horn. The sound of the spurs might be an amusing distraction on rides that seemed to last forever day after day, but they were generally used to control the motion of horses (and were dulled upon purchase so as not to punish the animal).

The Rides

Speaking of horses, one cowhand in each trail was in charge of the remuda, aka the grouping of about 100 or so extra horses, since each cowboy would usually exhaust two in a day's work. In other words, the fabled friendship between one man and one beast was essentially a Hollywood legend—literally and figuratively. John Wayne and James Stewart were known to use the same horse from one picture to the next, just as the characters they portrayed favored one animal as they saddled up and traveled from one town to the next. This was rarely the case in real life, although a particularly skilled horse might warrant some wistful comparative praise around the campfire at night.

The Grub

The campfire was always near the chuck wagon—a wagon equipped in the back with a drop door and two hinged legs that, when lowered, opened to a tall stocked box pantry—which usually rode out in front of the herd. You were pretty much guaranteed to find coffee brewing 24/7; you weren't guaranteed that it would be fresh. As for the food, it came from the limited stockpile the "pot wrangler," "dough belly" or whatever

CHOW TIME
Meals (below) offered a brief respite during the trail runs, a chance to trade tales, eat and rest up from the long days.

RIDE ON
Dakota cowboy Ned Coy (below right) shows off his "bucking bronco" skills circa 1888.

nickname the often-elderly cook had: cured bacon, flour, cornmeal, canned goods, lard, brown sugar, salt and sourdough for biscuits. Water could be found in a large cask at the side of the wagon, and fuel came courtesy of any source that might be available on the trail. The cook was the second in command—and therapist, dentist or barber when necessary. The Dutch oven, forks and plates were in the body of the wagon, right near all the bedrolls.

The Trail Rides

There'd be two per year, one when the grass first turned green and a second in the fall. The official trails headed up from Texas toward points farther north, where they would meet the railroad, and they headed farther west as America did. The cows first had to be branded and dehorned, have their tails bobbed and, for the males, castrated—practices that brought out the temper in both animal and man. The first days of the trail runs meant pushing the cattle to their limits in order to tire them out. A trail boss would hire about a dozen cowboys to shepherd 2,000 to 2,500 cattle, along with the cook and head of the remuda. Cowboys were paid $30 to $45 per month (all of $500 to $600 in today's money) for about four months of steamy 14-hour days, followed by nights where fear of stampedes or thieves made for great restlessness. Along the way, one would be confronted by Indians demanding payment to permit movement, or ranch owners wanting the same to allow passage over their land. A riverbank or stream could be incredibly dangerous; if not handled well, many cattle could die, and the cowboys would be responsible. The life, later romanticized lock, stock and barrel, could hardly have been more different from how the movies made it out to be. Later attempts to unionize the cowboys failed miserably.

"We have created the myth of the cowboy around the epitome of the rugged individualist; the reality is these were poorly paid wage workers," says Stephen Aron, PhD, a professor of history at UCLA. "For the most part, their dreams of independence, as understood by 19th-century men, were quite elusive."

The Towns

The longhorns had to be run up toward the Kansas City, Missouri, area, where they'd be loaded onto the trains that would take them east, usually to slaughterhouses in Chicago. (By 1870, 2 million animals were being processed there annually.) Abilene, Wichita, Dodge City and other Kansas towns that dotted the Plains became viable centers for rail workers and stockyards. They were also hotbeds of action, featuring saloons (Abilene had 32 of them in its small environs in 1870), places for gambling and prostitution—and a homicide rate 10 times that of New York City at the time. The men got paid and often as not blew a portion (or all) of their wages in town before starting the process all over again. And if they got too ornery, there was usually a sheriff around to knock 'em out cold with the butt of a Colt.

The Prime

The cattle runs of classic Western lore didn't last very long (even if, in Hollywood, they've gone on forever) in part because the 20 years after the Civil War saw all kinds of changes and challenges. A tick disease called Texas fever, carried by longhorns, wiped out a healthy portion of the domestic shorthorn stock. The depression of 1873 did investors no good. Too many cows on the trails shifted the demand and left the terrain overgrazed, and frigid winters followed by hot summers in the mid-1880s helped spell the end of the era, as did the evolution of the railroads. As Richard White, PhD, professor emeritus of American history at Stanford University, points out, "Once you get a railroad network, you don't need cattle drives."

When the dust settled, America was left with two cravings: for the taste of beef, and for the homespun tales of the mythical cowboy, a man with hard-won knowledge who had made it through the ultimate rite of passage—the cattle run.

"The cowboy becomes this universal figure of heroism and individualism," says John M. Findlay, PhD, professor of history at the University of Washington. "He's laconic and wise and he becomes this symbol of all of America. And when you get someone like John Wayne portraying him in the movies, it's a powerful image." ★

CLASSIC COWBOY
John Wayne was at his best in 1948's *Red River*. Director Howard Hawks had "Red River D" belt buckles made up for Wayne and others on the film; Wayne wore one of the buckles in nine of his other films.

The Homestead Act promised settlers 160 acres of land, provided that they'd guarantee that they would live on that land for at least five years. The going was rarely easy.

STRUGGLES OF THE LAND

THE SETTLERS WERE DETERMINED TO HEAD WEST, COME HELL OR HIGH WATER, NOT KNOWING THEY'D OFTEN FACE BOTH.

RUGGED BACKDROP
The classic Western film *The Searchers* presented the scenery of the West in all of its weathered, dangerous glory.

WHEN JOHN FORD WAS making his famed epic of the American West, 1956's *The Searchers*, he began by building what amounted to a "town" in the heated depths of Arizona's Monument Valley. For hours each day, between shots, John Wayne, his fellow stars and the hardworking crew members would deal with the harsh realities of life in the desert—albeit with food, water and other materials driven in. Later, moviegoers saw the raw beauty of the rocks, the terrible dangers of violence and life on the range and the simple times of hard-working families. It was the Wild West on display, Hollywood-style.

But about 100 years earlier, the homesteaders traveling in search of a better life had found a different kind of Wild West.

It was wild in its challenges to succeed in the face of irrigation shortages and poor soil, where you were apt to be less worried about murder than mudslides and monotony.

"The more blood-and-thunder tales take over the narrative [instead of] the much more mundane history—which is people trying to scratch a living from an unforgiving region," says University of New Mexico professor Durwood Ball. "It's more exciting to write about the U.S. Army marching across the Great Plains to New Mexico than to write about the operation of U.S. territorial government [in that area]."

Heck No, Must We Go?
Frontier diaries of the time paint a picture of the great reluctance of wives to leave friends, family and familiar lives behind and head west, often at the insistence of husbands with wanderlust. In a diary of Margaret Hereford Wilson—Gen. George S. Patton's grandmother—quoted in *Women's Diaries of the Westward Journey* by Lillian Schlissel, she writes, "Dr. Wilson has determined to go to California. I am going with him, as there is no other alternative.... Oh, my dear mother...I thought that I felt bad when I wrote you from Independence [Missouri]... but it was nothing like this." Making matters worse, as University of Washington professor John M. Findlay points out, by the time of the Wild West migrations, "A lot of the best land that has enough water for agriculture has been taken up. A lot of land is in precarious places, maybe the soil isn't great or they don't have a lot of rainfall."

Journeys Without End
People lured to the West from Europe had a lengthy passage to make before their

arrival. Even folks coming from the East found that the wagon route, promised to take about four months, took more like eight, a stretch where even the most serene-looking terrain will take on an ominous feel. Native Americans were often friendly, happy to trade and help, but they were just as often bitter, angry and violent, depending upon Army conflicts and the latest laws. Husbands who'd initiated these plans and left with high expectations found their disappointments equally high, relying on their wives for moral support and strength, given that death, disease and dread were wilderness companions. As Jane Gould Tourtillott recorded in her 1862 diary, "[My husband] Albert went fishing and caught two fish about as long as one's finger. His appetite is [unpredictable], he not being well.... In the afternoon, we passed a lonely, nameless grave on the prairie. It seems so sad to think of being buried and left alone in so wild a country, with no one to plant a flower or shed a tear o'er one's grave."

Arrive and Thrive?

The homesteaders who began new lives as farmers showed remarkable resiliency in the face of uncertainty and isolation. Famed pioneer Daniel Boone supposedly remarked that he wouldn't want to live within 20 miles of any neighbor. Nearly 100 years later, that great distance could feel stifling. In the recollections of Ethel Waxham Love, recorded in *The West: An Illustrated History* by Geoffrey C. Ward, she writes of life on her and her husband's Muskrat, Wyoming, sheep ranch in 1910: "The sheer aloneness of it is unique—never a light but one's own, at night." The Loves were the only inhabitants in an area the size of Rhode Island. Beyond work, there was often little to do. "You'd get an issue of a three-month-old newspaper and read it, front to back, 20 times," says Ball.

LONG VOYAGE
In the years after heading west, Dr. Benjamin Wilson (left) would find fortune and become the first mayor of Los Angeles. But his wife, Margaret, eloquently summarized the pains of leaving friends and family in the East in her diary.

RIDE ON
The wagon, aka the Prairie Schooner (below), was your integral means of Western transport. It took you out to the farm and also carried crops and supplies.

ON THEIR OWN
For the first generation after the initial move across the plains, women accepted their integral role in farm life; but as the U.S. become a more industrialized nation, young women flocked to cities to write their own destinies, away from the harder living.

The astonishing up-and-down swings the Loves faced on the path to decades of barely breaking even and staying alive would, again, redefine what "Wild West" could mean. The loss of thousands of sheep, the building of dams, winter storms following choking droughts, historic floods that destroyed property and led to bank foreclosures...then starting all over again, cleaning and managing to rebuild without government funds, building better dams, then a hailstorm, another dam burst, return to life as a paid sheep herder while raising a growing family and helping out whoever else passes by. And yet, the Loves kept their ranch 37 years and sent three kids to college.

"The West was a beautiful place," says Stanford University professor emeritus of American History, Richard White, "but in the 19th century, it's very often a tragic place—and in terms of what Americans think they're going to achieve, they don't achieve much."

Greener—But Less Green—Pastures
There is also a split, as the Wild West heads toward its close: The United States has inevitably shifted from a farming country to

an industrial one. The railroad is churning; cities are thriving; and youngsters who'd come west with families to farm are forging their own paths in cities such as Chicago and San Francisco. This is especially true of women, who sought to trade the oppression of life under the thumb of a demanding father on the farm for a shared room at the YWCA, a life as a wageworker and the incredible novelty of disposable income. "This is a time where American individuals can have a say and be masters of their own fate," says Findlay, "but in fact, the whole country was moving toward big cities and big business."

The growth away from the land continued for decades to come, and many settlers in

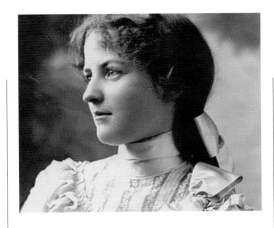

American cities came into town with their own determination, carrying something very important with them—the genes of their families, who had made the crossing on those long Great Plains roads in the first place, seeking a new life. ★

LOVE STORY
It took five years for John Love to win the hand of Ethel Waxham (left), and her journal of their life together tells an extraordinary tale of surviving western elements.

WOMEN'S WORK
Men were often the instigators of the moves to the West—but many women found ways to thrive.

The images of the West are indelibly clear—and exceedingly male. "There are very few cowgirls," says Stanford University professor Richard White. "There is this mostly all-male world...but then you had these farms, and it's hard to imagine a farm working without female labor. There, women play a central role." Granted, life on the farm could often be thankless, and boredom abounded. But one fascinating aspect of the Wild West and its draw to folks from the East is that men sought their American Dream, with many of them pulling up stakes almost on a lark. Women were by and large reluctant to go, but once there, some found their own path to bigger dreams. Several western territories allowed women to vote (unlike in the United States);

many women came to own boardinghouses and thrived in towns. As the new century approached, young women of the West explored new fates away from the kitchen and plow.

Also, history records that diligent women with pens, through diaries and journals, offered vivid pictures of that time and place, including day-to-day realities of life and love. Historian Sally MacNamara Ivey, one of the country's foremost collectors of journals that she archives under the name Sally's Diaries, shares a 1909 travel journal of a woman staying in a Montana hotel. As the woman wrote,"[Stayed] over last night, with roaches and bedbugs galore. Did not sleep much. They are like the saloon men: They may be alright, but I don't like the way they make their living."

Thousands of settlers made their way west along the Oregon Trail, encountering a host of troubles big and small along the way. Some travelers kept diaries that offer up unique insights into the journey.

TRIALS
ON THE
TRAILS

FRONTIER DIARIES OF ORDINARY TRAVELERS
WHO DOCUMENTED THEIR TREKS TELL THE EPIC TALES
OF SACRIFICE THAT HELPED MAKE THE WEST GREAT.

ON APRIL 9, 1853, DR. JOEL KNIGHT, his wife, Amelia, and their seven children began a journey from their Iowa home. Seeking a place with less severe weather, they were traveling to the virtually unknown land of the Oregon Territory. Like many other of the earliest homesteaders who headed for the West, Knight's wagon was one speck on a dotted line moving slowly toward a perceived sanctuary, without much understanding that each day would bring its own challenges, from dust and disease to mud and other menaces.

"...Traveled 12 miles today. We hear there are 700 teams on the road ahead of us. Wash and cook this afternoon," Amelia Stewart Knight wrote on May 12 of that year, in what has become one of Western history's greatest gifts: the frontier diaries of settlers heading across the Plains. On July 27, the family camped at what she described as boiling springs, "a great curiosity. They bubble up out of the earth boiling hot. I have only to pour water on to my tea and it is made.... I believe I never spent such an uneasy sleepless night in my life."

The diaries paint extraordinary pictures of expectations battling with realities and the remarkable toll they took, from one moment to the next. And yet the incredible act of simply getting through these challenges is a study in determination rivaling any account of individual achievement—mythical or otherwise—that the Wild West ever produced.

"We do have a lot of [historic material] that tells us, yes, it was very strenuous, and we also have stuff that tells us that people in the midst of it often thought, 'This is the most interesting thing I will ever do,'" says Patty Limerick, PhD, faculty director and board chair of the Center of the American West at the University of Colorado Boulder. "And some percentage of them said, 'I wish I could spend more time here.' It's not a huge percentage, but there are people in the overland diaries saying, 'If only we could just go climb that hill.'"

Weather, Water and Wear

Stewart Knight's diary is only one of many from men and women who thankfully took the time to record the journeys in their own words. Knowing now with 20/20 hindsight that, with time and better trails, and the construction of railroads and towns along the routes, things would improve immeasurably hardly eases the wonder of the earliest, hardiest accounts. "We have had all kinds of weather today," Stewart Knight wrote on May 16, 1853. "This afternoon it rained, hailed and the wind was very high. Have been traveling all the afternoon in mud and water up to our hubs. Broke chains and stuck in the mud several times. The men and boys are all wet and muddy. Hard times, but they say that misery loves company. We are not alone on these bare plains, it is covered with cattle and wagons." On June 1 she added, "Take us all together we are a poor looking set, and all this for Oregon. I am thinking while I write, 'Oh, Oregon, you must be a wonderful country.' Came 18 miles today."

For the Knight family, the journey would take a little more than five months, until September 17. A month later, Dr. Knight bought a claim in Clark County, Washington Territory, and the family settled into a new life. Behind them was a trip that saw the family's youngest child get scarlet fever and another child poison ivy, dreadful storms

that left everything and everybody soaked, wind that made lighting a fire for cooking (using buffalo dung for fuel) impossible, dirty drinking water that led to bouts of vomiting, and visits from Indians that were either necessary and helpful, or frightening and threatening.

And what the reader doesn't realize until the final entries is that Stewart Knight spent the entire way—over the rockiest terrain imaginable—pregnant, giving birth with Clark County finally coming into view. She concluded her diary by writing, "A few days later my eighth child was born. After this we picked up and ferried across the Columbia River.... Here husband traded two yoke of oxen for a half section of land with one-half acre planted to potatoes and a small log cabin and lean-to with no windows. This is the journey's end."

EARTHEN HOMES
Sod houses were common on the frontier, as they were cheap to build.

TOUGH GOING
Multiple challenges—
notably weather—met
the homesteaders once
they settled in the West.

FALSE PROMISES
Sadly for settlers, the
"best stock country"
land was taken up by the
railroads themselves.

Accounts of Record

Other accounts speak with greater bitterness
about the difficulty of the route, and the
toll it took. Several of the journals found
in historian Lillian Schlissel's *Women's
Diaries of the Westward Journey* have a
kind of cold dispassion about the death toll
that Schlissel suggests is the diarist's silent
protest against the very idea of leaving home

in the first place. The journal entries of
Cecilia McMillen Adams, who traveled with
her family from Illinois to Oregon in 1852,
are a simple, terrifying chronicle of miles
traveled and burials witnessed. "Passed 15
graves...made 13 miles," she wrote on July
11; the following day's entry read, "Passed
5 graves...made 15 miles." The reality of
watching new, unmarked graves spring up

while in the midst of pregnancy gave many women diarists a terrible unease.

Still more narratives contain a different emotional weight and a kind of wistful appreciation for all the effort, now that the task had been undertaken. Decades after McMillen Adams' entries, another woman detailed her family's trip from central Oregon to the state's coast and then, six months later, back again, all by wagon, and appears in a journal archived in the "Sally's Diaries" collection of renowned archivist Sally MacNamara Ivey. "We came on through the same old country, the scenes we came through last year with no change. But it refreshed one's memory and makes a person lonely and sad and wonder why one is just a wanderer on the face of the Earth when there is kindred and friends everywhere. We come on and camp on the very spot where our traveling companions of a year ago turned back and where we divided partnership. I wished they were here as I expect we could exchange many experiences since we parted."

These insights offer a perspective that no dime novel could ever touch. "I've often been asked if we did not suffer with fear in those days but I've said no, we did not have sense enough to realize our danger; we just had the time of our lives," wrote Nancy Hembree Snow Bogart, famously recalling her family's travels to Oregon in 1843 in her youth. "But since I've grown older and could realize the danger and the feelings of the mothers, I often wonder how they really lived through it all and retained their reason…. There were both deaths and births on the way, the dead were laid away in packing boxes, but could not be covered so deep but the prowling savage would exhume

> # "Before the railroad is completed, the overall migration can take six months. Once the railroad comes, it's six days from coast to coast."
>
> *Professor John Findlay*
>
> —◈◈◈◈—

them to get the clothes they were buried in, then leave the body for the hungry wolfe sic), that left bones to be gathered up and reinterred by the next company that passed along. All those things sorely taxed their powers of endurance."

And yet at the journey's end, the homesteaders' perseverance is a cause for wonder that retains a mythic life of its own. "There is in all this the sense of expectation of what the trip would be like that is just not accurate," says Limerick. "There are romances of prospect and romances of retrospect and they sometimes intersect and merge, but there is the romance of what people think they're going to get. And then when they don't get it, there's the looking backward and romanticizing."

Limerick continues, "The overland trail was very strenuous for the people who participated in it. It's a remarkable thing that so many people thought that they were having a historically significant experience, which caused them—even when really tired—to sit down and write." ★

Custer's Last Stand
at Little Bighorn
in 1876 resulted in the
general's decisive defeat.

CHAPTER FOUR

COWBOYS AND INDIANS, GUNS AND GLORY

The American cowboys of the Wild West have their roots in the Mexican *vaqueros*—ranch hands who rode horses, herded cattle and taught the tricks of the trade to their Northern counterparts.

THE
COWBOY
QUESTION

THE MOVIES ALWAYS TOLD US THAT THOSE ROUGH
RIDERS OF THE PLAINS WERE ACTION HEROES.
WELL, PARDNER, THE TRUTH GOES A BIT DEEPER.

C OWBOYS HAVE ALWAYS BEEN unique American heroes. A cowboy stands tough, carries a gun (we suggest you don't make him use it) and can probably rope a steer with the speed of a jackrabbit. He's the cattle handler of the Old West; we may not even know his real name—and we don't need to; he's a cowboy, and that's good enough.

What else do we know? Well, he can be rowdy as all heckfire, perhaps a result of all those long hours in the saddle, but he'll also respect a lady. And rest assured: A cowboy is as reliable as the sunrise and lives a life of constant daring and adventure, riding tall on his trusty horse, battling some of the greatest creatures in the American West: bedbugs and lice.

The truth of the matter is, if one were to suggest a profession more prone to exaggerated tales of valor than the cowboy, they'd be lying. It's not that the real cowhand wasn't brave and sure; it's that daily life wasn't all it appeared to be in those dime novels and, later on, in Hollywood movies.

"This is just brutal, brutal work, being thrown by horses, out in cold and terrible weather," says Richard White, Stanford University professor emeritus of American history. "For most of them, it's not a job anyone would ever aspire to—but mythically, this becomes the image of American masculinity."

We Can Understand How It Happened.

The stalwart horseman seems the picture of determination and independence—and, in many ways, he is. But where does the Wild West cowboy fantasy end and reality begin? Right here, on a truth scale of 1–10.

Cowboy Life Is One Thrill Ride After Another.

TRUTH SCALE

■■■■□□□□□

First of all, they weren't even called "cowboys." (For a time, that word literally meant boys who tended cows—or, in other circles, it was an insult, referring to the worst kind of outlaws or desperados.) They were cowpokes, cowhands, cowpunchers, cattlemen or drovers who became "cowboys" when novels and Wild West shows made the term cool. And the typical life of the cowhand included amazing stretches of nothing but ranch chores, with days fixing fences and evenings gambling or telling the same old tales. The rest of the year was spent on cattle runs that could take as long as four months, heading 1,200 miles away, riding 14 hours per day under the blistering sun, with bugs aplenty.

In truth, you hoped to avoid adventure, which could come in the form of ambushers, Native Americans or thunder or any other loud noise that could find you chasing a hundred frightened cattle in the middle of the night. "The [cowboys] go a little ways and then they try to cross a river, and it's very hard and very disorganized, and they get a little bit farther and it rains and it's muddy and hard to get across—and the question becomes: How did we ever get around to romanticizing this?" says University of Colorado Boulder history professor Patty Limerick. In other words, by the time you got to a town with your $100 pay, you were ready for a bath and a little bit of a different kind of adventure, followed by a lot of sleep.

The Cowboy Is the Very Image of Individuality.

TRUTH SCALE

■■■■■□□□□

Yes, a cowhand's life was, in one sense, his own (and the vast majority were men), but his employer was almost always a large company, which is something we don't usually see on film. "What's so weird about it is, at a time when Americans resisted wage work, cowboys are wageworkers," says White. "It's a stroke of genius that the symbols of American individualism

ALL THE FASHION
Woolly chaps (above) kept the cowboys warm while riding the range.

BUCKLED UP
Since anything from snakes to thunder could spook a horse, a cowboy had to not only trust his ability to calm his ride, he also had to constantly be on the lookout for trouble (far left).

SHOW AND TELL
The incredible roping skills fans saw in rodeos and Wild West shows was born out of the necessity for cowhands to practice their techniques incessantly in order to keep the many dangers at bay.

are going to be wageworkers, who very often work for large foreign corporations." It got bad enough that a group of cowhands got together to form a union. "They were disgusted with their treatment and wanted better wages and working conditions," says University of Washington professor John Findlay. A cowboy would usually start in the trade in his early 20s and, on average, be done within eight years. Increased success was rare, and it was only the older cattlemen and ranch owners who got the chance to grow up in the profession

and then say things like Gus does in *Lonesome Dove*: "The older the violin, the sweeter the music."

WHAT THE MOVIES TELL US

The Cowboy Is a Uniquely American Invention.

TRUTH SCALE

The other word for cowboys? "Buckaroos," which is the Americanized pronunciation of the Mexican *vaqueros*—which is what cowboys south of the border were called. The American cowboy also adapted chaps (necessary protection from the elements)—and hat styles, prairie vocabulary and even the use of horses—from Spain and Mexico and, to a certain degree, from Native Americans. Also, one in seven cowboys were African American (either from the Northeast or freed postwar slaves from the South), and one in seven was Latino.

WHAT THE MOVIES TELL US

Cowboys Are Skilled Horsemen.

TRUTH SCALE

■■■■■■■□□□

They'd better be: On the trail, there's lots of opportunity for cows to stray. Keeping the herd in line became a job and a half. Sometimes your horse had that great feel for the job, and sometimes the rider and horse actually had something of a bond, although most horses were owned by the company, not the cowboy. And most days on the trail, you'd go through two horses, with a "wrangler" keeping all the spare rides in line. Roping required immense skill—get a steer roped too fast with your hands in the wrong place, and you could lose a finger. You often saw great rope-trick skills, but the image of them came courtesy of Buffalo Bill's Wild West show. That helped create the myth of the cowboy that remains even today. (A certain NFL franchise is still called "America's Team," after all.) Says Findlay, "Cowboys were, in some ways, just a brief phase on the Great Plains, but because they're part of that last [phase of the] West and get romanticized, they get to live on forever." ★

THE ART OF MANLINESS

Frederic Remington and other artists created a cowboy vision that remains to this day.

Frederic Remington long struggled with his health and his weight, and the New Yorker originally headed to the West for the fresh air in 1880. A writer and illustrator by trade, it only took a few years in frontier lands for him to be caught up in the rugged romance of the place and its archetypes, and then apply his considerable skills to capturing the spirit for the folks back East. The results were historic: The long-standing vision of the cowboy on the Great Plains, staring at the endless American West horizon, comes straight from Remington's brush. To that, one can add novels such as Owen Wister's *The Virginian*, which concerned the unnamed cowboy title character, who was gun-ready and courageous but also courteous. Called a "son of a bitch" by the bad guy, he very famously unsheathed his pistol and replied, "When you call me that, smile." The book sold, as they say, like hotcakes—and between Remington, Wister, Zane Grey and others, the myth of the cowboy, so well-constructed by Buffalo Bill's Wild West shows, was forever guaranteed.

The idea that Indians on reservations could be trained as farmers was counter to their own traditions.

THE LAND WAS THEIRS

THE MOST FIERY DECADE OF THE 1800S SAW THE PERMANENT SHIFT OF THE NATIVE AMERICANS IN THE GREAT PLAINS, AS U.S. FORCES PUSHED THEIR WAY WESTWARD.

ON THE RUN
In a familiar-themed image, U.S. Cavalry troops are in hot pursuit of fleeing Native Americans.

THE PLAINS WERE OPEN—THAT'S what all the posters and flyers throughout the East and Europe said. Would-be homesteaders could head west and claim parcels of land for a song. The entire territory was ready for whatever you wished: farming, digging for gold, opening a town store and then, later on, building railroads. It was the great American movement writ large across the West.

Native Born

There was just one catch: the hundreds of Native American tribes who had made these lands their home for as long as 13,000 years and who had, for generations, welcomed explorers and intermingled with them. At times, they traded goods and formed alliances with non-Natives; at other times, they fought and killed (and were killed) because of territory, philosophy and religion—that's when the tribes weren't busy fighting among themselves. Diseases brought over from Europe wiped out thousands, perhaps millions of Native Americans.

But after the Civil War, when the West turned Wild, everything changed. Between army troops and Native tribes,

Sitting Bull (seated, center) appeared in some of Buffalo Bill's (standing, center) Wild West shows in 1885, and was amused by the mix of boos and cheers he received.

CUSTER'S LAST STAND
The death of Gen. Custer at Little Bighorn took on mythic proportions quickly, in literature, art and stirring reenactments at Wild West shows.

thousands were killed in hundreds of skirmishes. And then, when the smoke cleared, the railroad came through.

The Native Americans kept many of their languages, the customs they could hold on to, and a measure of pride, but they were settled more and more on reservations that, in time, grew smaller.

It took centuries for this seismic change to fully unfold. But no period seemed to spell this reversal for the Native Americans of the Great Plains more than the decade between 1876 and 1886, from Custer's Last Stand to Geronimo's surrender. And, of course, as it played out in real life, it also played out in Buffalo Bill's Wild West shows—often with Native Americans starring in the cast.

However one regards this incredible shift in Native American life—as inevitable, as tragic, as militarily justified, as forever difficult to justify—it remains a history that is still being written.

"Much that was done by mean white men was reported at Washington as the deeds of my people."

Apache Chief Geronimo

"For white men to fulfill their economic, political, cultural and social destinies, you had to take away the freedom of other people who were already in the West, particularly Native Americans," says Durwood Ball, professor of history at the University of New Mexico. "But when Native Americans are at the center of the story, it's very different. We're the aggressors and stealing their land and murdering men, women and elders.... And that's a very profound difference."

Setting the Stage

Texas, Oregon, Utah, California—the territories were, by the mid-19th century, available and rich and ripe for expansion, but the Native tribes were sprawled throughout. The land, to them, was not earmarked with boundaries. But the farmers and miners needed to set down their stakes and transplant the tribes. In the years before the Civil War, the U.S. government attempted to usher more tribes to the Pacific Northwest, where reservations waited, along with a new life: learning how to farm. Treaties were signed and many promises made.

In the Great Plains, the reluctance proved strong. Why move elsewhere when the buffalo were still roaming and a long-held way of life could easily continue? But as the settlers used more of the land and killed more of the bison, it became harder to keep to the lifestyle that went back generations.

The Civil War would tell the tale of whether slavery would move west along with the settlers. When the North won the war, expansion became a more determined way of life, and a frustrated United States government, tired of Indian insurrection, brought more firepower to bear in their push across the continent.

"Everyone else was moving west to settle, and at the same time was taking away the homes of those who were there," says James Diamond, director of the Tribal Justice Clinic and professor of practice at the University at Arizona in the College of Law. "There was no law other than the law of who had the biggest gun, and the only restrictions on settlement were whoever happened to have been there and had the bigger gun."

The Determined Push

The policy and the effort shifted after June 25, 1876. Gen. George Armstrong Custer, making a grievous tactical error at Little Bighorn, split his troops into three companies, unaware that several Indian nations—most notably, the great warrior Crazy Horse, leading his Oglala Sioux and Cheyenne warriors, and Sitting Bull and his Hunkpapa group of Teton Sioux—had gathered in that spot to confer about future strategy. When the attack was launched, Custer found himself outnumbered and outmaneuvered. He and his 250 troops were decimated, and a rally cry of avenging the

There are still close to 600 recognized Native American tribes, each with their own language and traditions.

PEACEFUL PROTEST
In the years before his death in 1904, Chief Joseph pleaded for a return of the native Nez Perce land.

tragic, martyred Custer became a motivation to push ahead with all force. What often gets lost, of course, is that Custer, his commanding officers and his troops had originally been the aggressors.

"For most of the 19th and 20th centuries, the story that explained Western conquest was Custer's Last Stand, which was about a besieged small group of white men, heavily outnumbered by Indians—and they, of course, are going to be slaughtered," begins Richard White, the renowned Stanford University history professor emeritus. "So now, all the Americans are doing is taking their just revenge. But it reverses the story—the Indians are being attacked. Custer is attacking, and it's their lands that are at risk, and that's the power of these stories. Why is it that the battles Americans remember are the ones where Americans are killed down to the last man? It's because that provides justification."

For the decade that followed, government policy and Army action led to an aggressive push to free the Plains of Native populations. Sitting Bull, Chief Joseph, Crazy Horse and Geronimo fought to retain their own way of life, in a setting already being overrun by settlers who were using the same resources for a different way of life. Shoshone, Cheyenne, Arapaho, Comanche, Sioux and others, undone by plagues, power and pressure, were forced to accept the movement to reservations. Assaults had long been taking place during the winter months, when the Natives were most vulnerable. And now the fighting was relentless. In 1886, the 48th Congress submitted a report accompanying a bill to push a railroad through the Great Plains, with language that stated: "The right of eminent domain in the federal government over the Indian Territory is the principle on which the bill has been constructed.... The Indian Territory is a part of the United States and subject to its jurisdiction."

Less than a year after Little Bighorn, a discouraged and beaten Crazy Horse surrendered; four months later, he was killed. Chief Joseph of the Nez Perce—a tribe that had long been on friendly terms with the white man—tried to keep the peace and be cooperative while not being taken advantage of, but the military pushed the tribe to war until Chief Joseph was supposedly compelled to declare, "I will fight no more forever." Sitting Bull first surrendered in July 1881, met Annie Oakley a few years later and then was famously part of the Buffalo Bill's Wild West shows in 1885; he was a star as well as a controversial attraction. But his great uneasiness with reservation policies and the fear of U.S. Indian agents that he was stirring up a movement among the Sioux led to him being shot and killed in 1890.

The Apache were the most formidable of warriors. But even their Chief Geronimo felt the need to surrender in 1884, only to escape with his ever-smaller band of troops,

AN END TO CONFLICT
The always-peaceful Nez Perce leader Chief Joseph was pushed to war, and, after months of flight, finally surrendered on October 5, 1877.

"Buffalo Bill kept alive the Wild West conflict theme, even as he worked for compromises."

Historian Richard W. Etulain

keeping the Army forces at bay for two years. By late 1886, Geronimo finally came in from the cold and set down his arms. For years, he was regarded in society as a star of the Wild West, a curiosity and an attraction, something that allowed him a living (though not the life he and his tribe had once known and enjoyed). Meeting with President Theodore Roosevelt in 1905, four years before his death, he asked for a chance to move his people back to Arizona, a request that was denied. Geronimo, Roosevelt said, was a "bad Indian," who had "killed many of my people."

The Aftermath

The final battle between Indian and U.S. Army forces, the Wounded Knee Massacre, on December 29, 1890, came with each side of the conflict tensely maintaining its position: Sioux forces under Chief Big Foot wavered between independence and defiance, and Army forces surrounded the Sioux and ultimately fired the first shot— which left as many as 200 Native forces dead, alongside 65 soldiers.

The battles took a tremendous toll on the Native populations, which, by 1890, were on reservations dotted throughout the West.

As University of Colorado professor Patty Limerick points out, plenty of Indians also managed to work with the Anglo population, as traders, guides or other professions—but the reality of this great shift remains, and the challenges continue today, more than 140 years after Custer's Last Stand.

"Natives deserve credit for maintaining agency and having a megaphone to press their case, often in courts or in courts of public opinion," says University of Washington professor John Findlay of efforts to maintain anything from land rights to economic independence. "They've made it clear they're not going away—and if people pay attention, there are really rich evocations of the Native experience. We have to pay closer attention to their stories." ★

THE PRIDE REMAINS
Native Americans keep up the struggle to control their destiny.

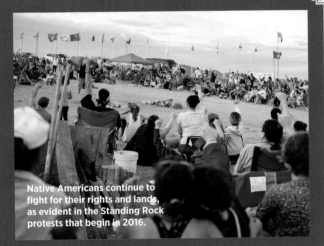

Native Americans continue to fight for their rights and lands, as evident in the Standing Rock protests that begin in 2016.

For Native Americans, the yearning for autonomy—in life and through the law—continues to be an operative goal, with Indian Civil Rights and Indian Self-Determination Acts meant to funnel better means of assistance. In many cases, they have thrived economically, but on the reservation, poverty and unemployment are constant. The struggle to keep their cultures intact has been a motivating force even today, as some of those same Wild West frustrations keep both sides apart.

"For most demographic socioeconomic groups, seeking the 'American Dream' has traditional obstacles. Indians have more significant obstacles because of historic discrimination and the impact of colonization on self-esteem, plus the reluctance to completely assimilate because it would wipe out their culture," says University of Arizona law professor James Diamond. "Others can [in theory] pick and choose the rate at which they want to assimilate; for Indians, it's more complicated. Assimilation means elimination of language and culture." And that, Diamond believes, is the death knell Native Americans wish to avoid, as they keep yearning for their own return to a truly American Dream. "There are still many places where they speak native languages," Diamond says. "They don't want that eliminated."

The dissent continues without any end in sight. The two Treaties of Laramie, in 1851 and 1868, were meant to keep Native nations on their own lands, with treaties broken many times. In 1980, the United States v. Sioux Nation of Indians Supreme Court case, which can be seen as something of an apology, ruled that tribal lands were taken illegally, with the tribes owed compensation plus interest. The interest is currently more than $1 billion. The Sioux continue to refuse the money. They want their land back instead.

A trio of Arizona cowboys, each armed with a couple of Col. Colt's Peacemakers.

SHOOTING STARS

THE WEST WAS A PLACE FOR WEAPONS OF MASS PRODUCTION—HERE ARE THE LONG SHOTS, BIG SHOTS AND HOT SHOTS OF THE ERA.

THERE WAS AN OLD SAYING out West in the 1850s that went something like, "God created men but Sam Colt made them equal." Given the propensity for violence in the 19th-century frontier, it seems apt enough. When Col. Samuel Colt (right)—among the richest men in America, thanks to a business acumen that included coining the marketing phrase "new and improved"—died in 1862 of gout, he'd already established the U.S. template (and the stubbornly protected patent) for the revolver. About 10 years later, his company would produce one of the most iconic guns of the West—threateningly named The Peacemaker. It's only one of a host of heavy-duty period firearms; here are 10 of the most renowned.

Sharps Rifle

WHY IT RATES This single-shot rifle, first designed in 1848, was the ultimate buffalo-hunting weapon, felling more of the beasts than any other firearm in the era. Chambered for powerful rounds and long ranges (as much as 1,500 yards), the 1874 model, available in several calibers and adopted by a number of international armed forces, was a favorite of the legendary Calamity Jane.

COOL FACTOR Some Civil War–era versions of the Sharps carbine had a built-in, hand-cranked grinder along the stock. You could, in theory, use the rifle to fell a bison or an enemy, and then grind your own coffee.

Colt Paterson

WHY IT RATES Introduced in 1836 as a .28-caliber model, and taking its name from the site of Colt's New Jersey factory, this was the first commercially sold multiple-chamber, revolving-cylinder firearm with a single barrel. The 1839 model introduced a more convenient reloading assembly. The pistols were popular among the Texas Rangers fighting Indians in the 1840s. But the gun may be as well-known for its single-action pluses as for its being central to an 1849 patent fight that Col. Colt won, securing gun-design rights through the mid-1850s.

COOL FACTOR The Paterson had a folding trigger, visible only when cocking the hammer.

Colt Model 1851 Navy Revolver

WHY IT RATES Colt sold some 215,000 of these light six-round .36-caliber cap-and-ball revolvers. They fit comfortably in a belt holster and were your fast friend during the days of Western expansion. A mechanical improvement over the Paterson, this was the gunmaker's first huge success in the trade, and he engraved the cylinder with a victorious Texas Navy battle scene. Doc Holliday and Robert E. Lee were among those counting this as a favorite.

COOL FACTOR When Wild Bill Hickok was killed during a Deadwood poker game, his Colt Navy Revolver was reportedly sold to help pay for burial expenses.

The legendary Henry starred along with Kevin Costner in *Dances With Wolves*.

The Henry 1860 Rifle

WHY IT RATES Breech-loading lever action, brass receiver, high rate of fire, 15-round magazine (with one more in the chamber)...this was the first iconic frontier rifle, straight from the brilliant mind of Benjamin Tyler Henry. Its infamy comes from it being the weapon of choice among Sioux and Cheyenne who won the day at Little Bighorn, but its fame comes from it being the rifle du jour throughout the Civil War, as small-but-steady production made it quite the in-demand model.

COOL FACTOR This is the rifle upon which the famed Winchester 73 was based, and it had its own starring role in movies such as *Dances With Wolves*, *True Grit* (both versions) and *Django Unchained*.

Remington 1858

WHY IT RATES Blame the Colt factory fire of 1864 for helping make the Eliphalet Remington & Sons model (which actually came out in 1861) a Union Army staple during the Civil War—and a favorite among officers in the years afterward. The single-action, six-shot, percussion revolver was accurate, powerful and durable, with three separate models, each boasting improvement tweaks. The 1868 version began offering metallic cartridge conversion.

COOL FACTOR In 2012, Buffalo Bill Cody's Remington 1858 sold at auction for $239,000. He'd used it from 1868 to 1906, ultimately surrendering it to his ranch foreman with a note reading, "It never failed me."

Springfield Model 1866

WHY IT RATES Breech-loading rifles—guns loaded from a rear chamber—carried great advantages for anyone under attack, and the refinement in Springfield's 1865 model tripled or quadrupled the number of rounds per minute you could fire. The only rub was, breech system parts were small and unreliable, and the 1866 model was developed in quick order. This much more widely used "second-Allin" iteration became the basis for rifles that would be carried by U.S. troops well beyond the war, and into the West.

COOL FACTOR Buffalo Bill Cody earned his nickname thanks to a bison-shooting contest he won using this gun, which he nicknamed Lucrezia Borgia, after the notoriously ruthless Italian noblewoman.

FIRE FIGHT
The Springfield was a big asset in Indian skirmishes.

Smith & Wesson No. 3 Revolver

WHY IT RATES Well...it was good enough for Annie Oakley. It was introduced with a bang in 1870, and Little Sure Shot used three of these single-action top-break service revolvers in her incomparable career as a star markswoman. The six-round cylinder pistol was also internationally popular, with models including the .44 Henry rimfire and .45 Schofield, named after Maj. George Schofield, who modified the design to better suit the cavalry's needs.

COOL FACTOR Variations on the three Russian models became staples of Russian Empire conflicts in the 1870s, and Smith & Wesson sold the No. 3 in Japan, Italy, Romania and Spain.

Colt Single Action Army

WHY IT RATES The standard military service revolver in the U.S. through 1892, the extraordinarily popular Peacemaker would also be among the most famed firearms of the West. A six-shot gun that first came to market in 1873, the SAA was developed in versions with 30 different calibers and several barrel lengths, and whenever Colt seemed ready to take it off the market, demand rose.

COOL FACTOR Gen. George Patton, who began his military career in the horse cavalry, favored an ivory-handled Peacemaker engraved with his initials. And did Wyatt Earp carry a Buntline Special Peacemaker into the O.K. Corral? Nope, but that Wild West myth persists.

Victor Mature's Doc Holliday brandishes a double-barrel shotgun in *My Darling Clementine*.

Winchester 1873

WHY IT RATES Is it "The Gun That Won the West?" If not in fact, then in fiction, thanks to Hollywood's insistence on featuring this repeating-arms rifle with a 24-inch barrel that grew out of the famed Henry. Winchester sold some 720,000 of these, including the shorter carbine model, each with a powerful .44-40 cartridge, toggle-link action, sliding dust cover and a crescent-shaped butt plate.

COOL FACTOR It's the most celebrated Western-film rifle. John Wayne added a large loop lever to his so he could twirl it, pistol-like, in 1939's *Stagecoach*, and James Stewart searched relentlessly for his in 1950's *Winchester '73*.

Double-Barrel Shotgun

WHY IT RATES Like Clint Eastwood's "Man With No Name," this is a gun without a name—or, rather, it's the scion of many manufacturers. Introduced in 1875, the breech-loaded, side-by-side (or over-under) weapon became a favorite of stagecoach drivers due to its close-range power. Used with a purpose-built shell or cartridge with shots or pellets, it was also preferred by skeet shooters and hunters, and a classic in films.

COOL FACTOR That's Henry Fonda's Wyatt Earp using a double barrel in 1946's *My Darling Clementine* and Paul Fix's Sheriff Watson using his in 1965's *The Sons of Katie Elder*, among too many Western appearances to count. ★

Theodore Roosevelt was captivated by the frontier life during his first visit in 1883.

FRONTIER PRESIDENT

THEODORE ROOSEVELT CURED PERSONAL TRAGEDY BY EMBRACING THE ROUGH LIFE OUT WEST. AFTERWARD, HE—AND AMERICA—WOULD NEVER BE THE SAME.

By writing *The Virginian*, Roosevelt's friend Owen Wister would create the cowboy archetype.

THEODORE ROOSEVELT SAW HIS entire life unravel in 12 hours on a February day in 1884. The man whose career as president would one day see his face among Lincoln's, Washington's and Jefferson's on Mount Rushmore, lost his mother to typhoid fever at 3 a.m. on February 14; 11 hours later, Roosevelt's wife, who'd given birth to the couple's first daughter two days prior, died of an undiagnosed kidney ailment. A faithful diarist, Roosevelt marked a giant "X" in his journal on that day, and added only, "The light has gone out of my life."

And yet, the actions he took as a result of this lowest ebb did as much to create the Western myth as anything a Tombstone gun battle or a Hollywood cowboy film ever did. Leaving his infant daughter in the care of his sister, Roosevelt, then a New York State assemblyman and son of an elite, upper-class family, fled to the Dakota Territory, invested thousands of dollars in one ranch and thousands more to build another and burrowed in, hoping the isolation and a measure of hard work would cure his deep emotional wounds. It ended up doing more than that; in his self-imposed seclusion, he found encouragement, meaning and the sense of individuality he'd one day become known for. The trip reframed his life and career on the path to becoming America's first Stetson-wearing "cowboy president"—a mythologized image that has only flourished in the years since.

"In the 1870s, the 'cowboy' is regarded as a somewhat disreputable figure in our culture," says Stephen Aron, PhD, a professor of history at UCLA. "And the kind of resuscitation of the image, or really the creation of the image, begins with Theodore Roosevelt."

By his own account, Roosevelt's early days in the Dakotas were meant to be a retreat from terrible memories, and political ambitions that had also been dashed following his discontentment with the 1884 presidential campaign. Writing to a friend that he would "never become reconciled to his loss nor expect to find happiness again," he found solace on horseback among like-minded fellows, and began to refer to himself as a cowboy. Doing so did not win him any friends among the ranch hands whose hard toil was a 180-degree counter to the way Hollywood later viewed the spurs-jangling hero.

A Man Apart
"Roosevelt is an interesting character because by the descriptions of him, he's more of a toy cowboy," says Richard White, PhD, professor emeritus of American history at Stanford University. "He did participate in a roundup, but [a prominent area official] just disparages him." In an area where respect must be earned, Roosevelt is a Harvard-educated, somewhat effete Easterner who, like his college friend, writer Owen Wister, is regarded as something of a square peg.

But his admiration for all those who worked for "the sheer love of adventure" became intoxicating. At first, the frontier was his quiet, sad sanctuary. "Nowhere does a man feel more lonely than when riding over the far-reaching, seemingly never-ending plains; and after a man has lived a little while on or near them, their very vastness and loneliness and their melancholy monotony have a strong fascination for him," he wrote. But in time he started to embrace the exhilaration of his ranching life. And the

ALLY OF NATURE
The president and "practical forester" set aside more national park land than all his predecessors combined.

faces of his companions suggested to him "dangers quietly fronted and hardships uncomplainingly endured."

Tests of Will
But Roosevelt's reputation would never have flourished had he not eventually faced dangers himself. Confronted by a bully who

taunted him one night in a hotel in nearby Mingusville, the slighter-built Roosevelt surprised his tormentor with a slam to the jaw that knocked him down and—after he'd hit his head on the bar—out. In a later incident, Roosevelt reportedly went after a group of outlaws who had stolen a boat from his ranch, tracking them relentlessly through dangerous streams and Indian territory until he'd brought them to justice. These and other smaller victories in hunting expeditions earned Roosevelt the one notch on his belt he truly valued: the respect of men he'd hoped to embrace as peers. One ultimately called him "a Westerner at heart [with] the makings of a real man." Granted, his experience wasn't full of wonders; severe winter weather wiped out a large percentage of his herd. But the Dakotas became the balm Roosevelt needed to return home renewed.

Leaving the ranches for New York in 1886, he resumed his political career and rose through a series of appointments. He resigned his post as assistant secretary of the Navy under President McKinley in order to fight in the Spanish-American War and helped recruit the Rough Riders that would seal his standing as a figure who could connect the Eastern intellectuals with the more battle-tested, wily Westerners and bring victory to the U.S. Accepting the thankless task as vice president for McKinley's second term, he rose to the presidency when McKinley was assassinated. Of all his accomplishments in a little under eight years, his record as a booster of conservation and protector of federal land and wildlife—a notion tied to his love of the West—remained his proudest.

"Just the fact that we have national forests" speaks to his accomplishments, according to Patty Limerick, PhD, faculty director and board chair of the Center of the American West at the University of Colorado Boulder. "He also had the first White House conference on conservation."

From his time in the West onward, Roosevelt walked the walk and talked the talk of the individualism the West represented.

A PRACTICAL FORESTER
(A subject that had attention all through Mr. Roosevelt's Presidency.)

Perhaps no incident captured that better than the 1912 presidential election, which found him running as an independent candidate in the Progressive "Bull Moose" Party. On a stop in Milwaukee, Roosevelt was shot in the chest in an assassination attempt. Realizing the wound wasn't life-threatening, he refused immediate medical treatment and instead gave a 90-minute speech while blood poured onto his shirt, beginning with the words, "Ladies and gentlemen, I don't know whether you fully understand that I have just been shot, but it takes more than that to kill a Bull Moose." It would be difficult to concoct a more telling tale about both Western truth and myth in Roosevelt than that.

"Most of us who'd just been shot would not just put our hand over the bullet wound and go on giving our speech," says Limerick. "So there's some degree with just thinking that's a different kind of person." ★

The legendary Buffalo Bill Cody sits on horseback in front of tents for his Wild West show, circa 1900.

CHAPTER FIVE

TRUE-LIFE MYTH MAKERS

Wild Bill Hickok's outsize reputation suffered when he accidentally killed his own deputy in Abilene, Kansas.

THE
TALLEST
TALE
OF ALL

AN 1867 MAGAZINE STORY TURNED WILD
BILL HICKOK INTO A HUGE STAR—AND GAVE
HIM A REPUTATION HE'D NEVER OUTLIVE.

RISING TO FAME
The wildly exaggerated tales of Hickok in *Harper's* (above) helped elevate him to star status.

HANGING UP HIS GUN
After accidentally killing his deputy (top), Hickok never engaged in another gun battle.

G EORGE WARD NICHOLS, AUTHOR of one of the most spectacular and popular magazine stories of the 19th century, watched the man he'd come to write about as he galloped with ease, grace and a kind of exciting fury into Springfield, Missouri. The man had, as Nichols recalled, "the handsomest physique I had ever seen." Around his shoulders, a deerskin shirt hung jauntily. The breadth and depth of his chest were remarkable, and though his expression was gentle, his was a face not to be trifled with.

He was James Butler "Wild Bill" Hickok, the famed mountain scout, Civil War hero, Union spy and—most importantly to the readers of the February 1867 issue of *Harper's New Monthly Magazine*—a killer of hundreds of men. That list included Davis Tutt, the gambler he'd shot days earlier over money and women, in what history would record as the first-ever quick-draw Wild West duel.

"'They say Bill's wild. Now he isn't any sich thing,'" Nichols quoted Hickok's friend, known without any irony as "Captain Honesty," in the story, with words written in quaint Plains-speak. "'I've known him goin' on ter ten year, and he's as civil a disposed person as you'll find hear-abouts. But he won't be put upon.'"

Hickok already had a deserved reputation by the time the admiring Nichols came to Springfield to meet him in person. (Among other things, he told Nichols the tale of his killing 10 notorious men single-handedly, including McCanles Gang leader David McCanles.) But it would be hard to imagine a more fateful meeting of man and magazine.

Harper's had a rabid following back East, and in one fell swoop, Hickok—sporting a couple of Colts and one motor mouth—talked his way to legendary status, and a name to rival dime-novel favorites Kit Carson and Davy Crockett. It was the summation of his boyhood dream: He'd read those tall tales as a kid, and now he himself was a star.

But in those days, 150 years before the Kardashian era of the internet, Hickok's notoriety carried consequences. Boasting of your killing prowess tends to make you a marked man, and Hickok, as author Tom Clavin wrote in the biography *Wild Bill*, would spend the remainder of his life—all of 10 years—walking down the centers of streets and sitting with his back to the wall to protect himself. He'd frequently enlarge the stories he'd told Nichols to anybody who'd listen—in effect, becoming the legend—but could never live up to the high status he'd given himself.

Real Deal

Perhaps that was because, as many pointed out in the wake of the article's thrilling reception, Hickok was not quite the killer he'd made himself out to be. An unrivaled sharpshooter with an uncanny ability to split a bullet on the edge of a dime, Hickok's boasts that, among other acts, he'd once killed 50 Confederate soldiers with 50 bullets, brought detractors out of the woodwork. While acknowledging his sometime heroism and the enormous risk of getting on his bad side, folks resented the supposed length of his résumé.

"There's a long history of this that goes back to mountain men and braggadocio and the fact is that they are famous liars, and the one thing they could do is tell fantastic stories," says Richard White, PhD,

"I thought his the handsomest physique I had ever seen. In its exquisite, manly proportions, it recalled the antique."

George Ward Nichols, on Wild Bill Hickok

a professor emeritus of American history at Stanford University. "At first they tell the stories to each other, but then when they get picked up, it gets emblazoned onto people like Buffalo Bill Cody and onto cowboys. It's a whole kind of Western narrative of exaggeration, which was then picked up in the Eastern press."

No sooner had the story run than local newspapers began shooting holes in the claims Nichols made, and his descriptions of the residents of Springfield as "strange, half-civilized people...men and women dressed in queer costumes.... These men were temporary or permanent denizens of the city, and were lazily occupied in doing nothing." The dichotomy of these citizens seen alongside the handsome Hickok—whose horse, Nelly, was so smart she'd wink at his inside jokes—was too much for many justifiably angry locals. Not long after the story ran, a chastened Nichols left the writing profession.

Living the Tale

For Hickok, however, the story became the impetus to live off the wealth of reputation.

Starting in the late 1860s, he was elected marshal of several Kansas towns, each of which made good use of his skills. In many cases, his name alone was enough to keep order, but his duties didn't stop him from gambling and carousing. In Abilene, he established himself as what would later be seen in Hollywood as the definitive proud, principled and, when pressed, hot-tempered lawman. He inspired more enduring stories when he befriended a man passing through town, who turned out to be noted gunslinger John Wesley Hardin. After Hardin killed a man for snoring, Hickok sought him out, but the outlaw had already made a quick exit.

Hickok's luck officially waned when he tussled with Abilene saloon owner Phil Coe. When the braggart Coe claimed he could "kill a crow on the wing," Hickok was said to have replied with a line that, whether actually spoken or not, endures forever: "Did the crow have a pistol? Was he shooting back? I will be."

The two men took to firing, and in the process of mortally wounding Coe, Hickok accidentally also killed one of his own men,

UNLUCKY HAND
The killing of Hickok by Jack McCall has been depicted in lithograph, film, television, literature and reenactment.

Special Deputy Marshal Mike Williams, who'd been heading his way to help.

Fired from the job in Abilene after the incident, a terribly remorseful Hickok slid downward. Drinking became another profession, as did acting in some of the Wild West shows of his longtime acquaintance, Buffalo Bill Cody. It was a match made in celebrity heaven, but the reality was hellish. Cody never used real bullets in the show; a frequently drunk Hickok loaded them anyway, scaring everybody involved. "Cody tried to bring him in, but he was just incorrigible," says White.

And then, in an ending that was as fit for film as could be, Hickok—his eyesight fading and marksmanship less certain—landed in Deadwood, South Dakota, where he came in contact with a drifter named Jack McCall. Did McCall have a score to settle with the famed gunman? The motive was never quite clear, but one midsummer afternoon in 1876, he found Hickok in a saloon playing cards, uncharacteristically sitting with his back to the door. McCall shot him in the back of the head; later on, he reportedly said he'd shot the gunslinger that way because, "I didn't want to commit suicide." Hickok's last poker hand, with two black aces and two black eights, later came to be called the dead man's hand. McCall was hanged for the crime.

But like any great Wild West tale, the spin has never stopped. Hickok's life, as it were, has been told through movie portrayals by the likes of William S. Hart, Gary Cooper, Charles Bronson, Jeff Bridges and Luke Hemsworth. Fellow legend Calamity Jane long claimed that the two were once married. Separating the truth from the myth is a project in itself, and quite the challenge. But thanks to a magazine story that blazed a trail across the country, an enduring hero was born, and remains.

"We have this archetype in our history of the American West of the gunfighter, the lone gunman, the man who goes his own way and is confident that he's going to set things to right," Clavin once said. "Hickok was the prototype of that." ★

STAR POWER
In 1995's *Wild Bill*, Jeff Bridges was cast as the title character; Keith Carradine plays fellow legend Buffalo Bill Cody.

This image portrays
Wyatt Earp as a
model citizen.

WYATT EARP'S DOUBLE LIFE

WAS HE HERO, HORSE THIEF OR BOTH? NO WESTERN FIGURE'S LEGACY INSPIRES MORE DEBATE.

I N THE 1931 BIOGRAPHY *WYATT EARP: Frontier Marshal*, writer Stuart N. Lake perfectly summed up his subject, and the man's era, this way: "The Old West cannot be understood unless Wyatt Earp also is understood." Lake defended his point by painting Earp—the quintessential Wild West lawman, and central figure in 1881's Gunfight at the O.K. Corral—as a titanic hero and a necessary face of justice in a rough and reckless world.

"He no longer stands simply [as] an unbelievably courageous figure distinguished by fabulous feats of arms and an extraordinary domination over men," Lake wrote in a manuscript awash in hyperbole. "In true perspective he is recognized as something more, as an epitomizing symbol."

But Lake got one thing wrong. It's not Wyatt Earp "the man" who is the defining symbol of the Old West; it's Earp "the myth."

We can see that myth so clearly from the TV shows and movies that are based on him. Earp is a stalwart sentry, clad in black with a shining badge, patrolling the dusty streets of Tombstone, Arizona, looking as reliable as the sunrise alongside brothers Morgan and Virgil, and his tragically tubercular best friend, Doc Holliday. He will always save the day.

But what about the man? People have argued the details of his life for decades. He was a feared and resolute peace officer... and an unprincipled gambler and con man who got into any number of scrapes in his day. Did he and his cohorts defend the town's honor at their famous gunfight... or did they shoot some of their opponents without provocation? Was Earp a hero, or a horse thief?

In fact, Earp was something greater than both of those things: He was the ultimate opportunist. In the right place at the right time, he pursued heady ambitions and knew success and failure, spending many days guarding the jail doors and a bunch of nights behind them. But toward the end of his days, feeling the itch to benefit from his dramatic life through Hollywood, he allowed Lake to tell his tale, and then died not long before the writer turned him into the most fabled figure for good the West ever knew.

A Life in Full

Anyone who maintains an opinion of Wyatt Earp's life would at least agree on one thing: However it's characterized, it is something epic. Inheriting a sense of wanderlust from their ever-on-the-move father, Wyatt and his brothers grew up in Illinois and Iowa and then settled in San Bernardino, California, in the waning days of the Civil War. Wyatt drove wagons, worked for the Union Pacific and gambled with some success as the family soon headed back home to Illinois.

A pattern was emerging: As word of new boomtowns and opportunities arose in places out West, Wyatt would go searching for a chance to cash in and make his mark. In stops from Lamar, Mississippi, to Prescott, Arizona, to California and back, he traveled, visited family, found work as a constable in Lamar (beating his brother Newton in the election in 1870), got married to a woman who sadly died young of typhoid, and then made his way into Indian territory. An arrest for stealing horses made Wyatt's wanderlust a necessity and he escaped the law by heading to Kansas, spending some time

TALL TALES
Author Stuart N. Lake later admitted he'd only met with Earp six to eight times while creating his "firsthand" account.

behind bars along the way for vagrancy and soliciting prostitutes.

But he also had a talent for keeping the peace, which he did in Dodge City and Wichita, Kansas, though his police job in the latter ended after he beat up the political rival of his boss. He also had a thirst for commerce and in 1879, when he heard word of a silver boom in the newly founded town of Tombstone, it seemed like the opportunity of a lifetime.

Gunning for Fame

Of course, as we know from history, there was one problem. Tombstone's cattle-rustling Cowboys—including Ike and Billy Clanton, Tom and Frank McLaury and Billy Claiborne—were used to getting away with their illegal activities. Meanwhile, newcomers like Wyatt, his brothers Virgil and Morgan, and Wyatt's close pal Doc Holliday were trying to consolidate profit and power in town through politics, buying into businesses and as law enforcers.

A couple of years of stagecoach robberies, killings, investigations, arrests, deals made, deals broken, accusations, pistol whippings, bad-mouthing in the press and constant threats to kill the Earps took their toll, and led to an October 26, 1881, date with destiny at an empty lot near Fremont Street in town. In 30 seconds, 30 shots were fired between the Earps and Holliday and the Cowboys, with the Earps getting the better of their opponents. There were three deaths (among the Cowboys), two injuries (among the Earps) and some escapes. The only figure who emerged unhurt and who didn't have to go on the run was Wyatt Earp.

Charged with murder by Ike Clanton, the Earps stood trial and were ultimately acquitted of the crime, although not without some star witnesses claiming the Cowboys didn't even have guns with them. (That claim always annoyed Wyatt, since his brothers had been shot.) Despite the verdict, controversy continued, and when Virgil was shot and Morgan killed in retribution, Wyatt's murderous revenge received national attention. The gunfight and the vendetta would be the seed Stuart Lake used to create Wyatt Earp's legendary status.

ON THE TOWN
A well-dressed Earp stands alongside a stately Packard during his days in Los Angeles.

Unsettled Settler

But immediately after the gunfight, Wyatt was back on the run. In San Francisco, he reunited with Josie Marcus, who'd reportedly been the common-law wife of Tombstone sheriff Johnny Behan; Behan had testified against the Earps after the Corral battle. Wyatt and Josie would be together for the next 46 years, always seeking a path to fortune. The urge took them to a gold rush in Idaho, a real estate boom (and some horse racing interests) in San Diego, Wyatt's infamous refereeing of an 1896 heavyweight boxing match in San Francisco that many claimed he'd fixed, a gold rush (and saloon ownership) in Nome, Alaska, more gold and another saloon in Nevada and finally, mining claims in Vidal, California, along with summers in Los Angeles. Through the 1910s and 1920s, as Hollywood studios were built and the Western became the most popular genre in town, Wyatt sought a payday for his life story to be told either in print or on screen. No one was biting, even though big-screen

heroes played by Tom Mix and William S. Hart resembled the real-life Wyatt.

"The movies then were mostly feeding on other movies and on dime novels, but Earp's story is at this point really difficult to work with," says Richard White, PhD, professor emeritus of American history at Stanford University. "He's somebody who has been thrown in jail. He's probably a horse thief. He's a murderer and an enforcer in houses of prostitution and he's well known as a crooked referee in prizefights. So he's a colorful guy, but to have him become the emblem of law and order in the West is pretty astonishing."

But the timing was fortuitous. Lake, who had once run public relations for a Theodore Roosevelt presidential campaign, began a correspondence with Earp, collecting anecdotes and seeking positive comments from acquaintances whom the lawman had known during his frontier days. Citing those compliments, Lake wrote to Earp in November 1928, "I think your record is the finest of any man who

Virgil

Wyatt

Morgan

helped to tame the frontier. [Your friends] all subscribe to my belief that whatever was done by you was in the interests of the right." A flattered Earp wrote back at one point, "For my handling of the situation at Tombstone, I have no regrets. Were it to be done over again, I would do exactly as I did at that time."

Wyatt Earp died of kidney failure in 1929. Two years later, Hollywood movies were glorifying gangsters and Western lawmen, the United States was deeply mired in the Depression and everybody yearned for a stalwart hero. Into this cultural milieu rode the tale of *Wyatt Earp: Frontier Marshal*, about a man who made the world safer with a pistol and a conscience. Lake wrote his book as a first-person narrative, rightly thinking it would be more dramatic. It made a fortune.

Scourge of the West

The rest is revisionist history. Two films, both called *Frontier Marshal*, came out in 1934 and 1939, and John Ford's classic *My Darling Clementine*, also based on Lake's

book and starring Henry Fonda and Victor Mature, was a 1946 box office smash. And after the 1957 release of *Gunfight at the O.K. Corral*, with Burt Lancaster and Kirk Douglas, nobody much cared if the incident actually took place somewhere else. In all the films, the Earps are the good guys; the idea that they could be anything else—even flawed—fell away from national consciousness. And through Wyatt Earp, the myth of the West lived on.

"I guess at some point, [though it's] not going to happen, it would be nice if they could be permitted to be full human beings, right?" says Patty Limerick, PhD, professor of history and chair of the board of the Center of the American West at the University of Colorado Boulder. "Going into historical memory, this character is basically about as interesting as a stick figure," she observes. "It's just predictable: 'And there he goes again. He's blazing the way with both guns.' But at a certain point, you're probably wondering, is that all there is? And no, that's probably not all there is." ★

In hundreds of dime novels, honor and virtue motivated Buffalo Bill's heroic actions.

THE ONE TRUE GENIUS

NOBODY SHAPED AND PROMOTED THE LEGEND OF THE WILD WEST MORE THAN BUFFALO BILL.

BUFFALO BILL'S WILD WEST

"THE MAZE"
THE MOST ANIMATED EQUESTRIAN SPECTACLE EVER SEEN. A GORGEOUS MOVING PICTURE IN WHICH OVER 300 HEROIC HORSEMEN PARTICIPATE

GLOBAL SUCCESS
Posters promoting his many extravaganzas made Cody a household name worldwide.

THEY'D BEGIN WITH AN EMPTY lot, or perhaps a racetrack or baseball diamond; seats were unfolded for 15,000 good folks surrounding an outdoor area almost exactly the size of a football field. And then...the day would come, with the paying customers rushing to sit and anticipation hanging thick in the air, until: A charge was sounded. Horses started racing across the lawn, 100 of them, even 200, with riders twirling ropes high in the air, and others shooting pistols; some were Indians, some were soldiers, many were cowboys, and a sense of enormous celebration moved like a wave across the grounds.

Then through the throng, with the band hitting a crescendo, came a lone figure on horseback, dressed in ceremonial garb, and now the crowd rose in appreciation. For here was the man they'd all come to see, the one who showed the world that this was truly the West, a place of adventure, danger and derring-do, where you could make your name in the wilderness.

This was the promise delivered by William F. "Buffalo Bill" Cody, and he sold it by the yarn. There would ultimately be 1,500 dime novels written about his exploits, and while most of the stories were lies or exaggerations, they perpetuated a legend he promoted better than anybody in American Western history. It all led to the creation of Buffalo Bill's Wild West, a spectacle that toured the world and brought him unparalleled fame from 1882 to 1916. Without Buffalo Bill, the beloved cultural figure known as the cowboy would simply not exist. It's not hyperbole to say that Cody made the myth of the West come alive, and that in time, the myth sadly marched right on past him.

"He is probably the only true genius the Wild West ever produced," says Richard White, PhD, professor emeritus of American History at Stanford University. "He'd been a hunter, a scout and a soldier, but what he realized very quickly was that there was far more money to be made in representing these things than in actually doing them. And so he begins to inhabit his own representation. And I think at the end, even Buffalo Bill had a hard time keeping apart Buffalo Bill the man and the character."

Scout's Honor

Like his friend Wild Bill Hickok, Cody's early life set a strong foundation for his legend. In 1853, when he was 7, Cody's father was stabbed at a political meeting in Kansas for speaking out against slavery, suffering injuries he'd never fully recover from. A few

SHOOTING STAR
Cody's friend Thomas Edison made the film *The Little Sure Shot of the West*, celebrating the prowess of Wild West show star Annie Oakley.

years later, to help support the family, Cody reportedly began to take on a number of occupations, from mounted messenger to Pony Express rider to trapper. After two years in the Union Army during the Civil War, he married Louisa Frederici, and in 1867, while working for the Kansas Pacific Railway as a buffalo hunter supplying meat for workers, he entered a buffalo-shooting contest against Bill Comstock. Cody won the match, earning a nickname that would last a lifetime.

His most suitable calling was as a territory scout, a man who rode ahead of any party of civilians or troops to pick out trails, locate camping grounds and spot any dangers. During the four years he spent scouting in the Army from 1868 to 1872, he built a reputation for incomparable skill, being an instrumental presence during 16 battles of the Indian Wars, while also famously scouting a hunting party for Grand Duke Alexei Alexandrovich of Russia.

Writ Large

All that experience would have been enough for any robust autobiography, but in 1869, Cody met the publisher Edward Judson, who wrote under the pseudonym Ned Buntline. After soaking up Cody's many real (and tall) tales, Buntline wrote the popular novel *Buffalo Bill, the King of the Border Men*, in December 1869, which was turned into a play in 1872. Later that year, when Buntline wrote a drama called *Scouts of the Prairie*, Cody co-starred in it as himself, and was bitten by the performance bug. For the next 10 years, he split his time between being a scout, Indian fighter and showman, as more novels spun tales of his many adventures. Most famously, in 1876, after the death of Gen. George Armstrong Custer at the Battle

"He is the smartest of [all frontier figures] and he gets control of the myth, and turns himself into a hero not only in the U.S. but in Europe."

Professor Emeritus Richard White

of Little Bighorn, Cody joined a Nebraska Indian raid where he killed and scalped the Cheyenne chief Little Hand; soon after, he returned to the stage quite literally holding the "first scalp for Custer."

It was that extraordinary scene and many others that Cody would reenact, starting in 1883, in his traveling show called Buffalo Bill's Wild West. Cody never permitted his circus-like spectacle to be referred to as a "show," wanting his audiences to regard it as the real deal. For the remainder of his life, Cody expanded the attraction and influence of his presentation, winning fame throughout the U.S. and into Europe. He gave a royal command performance in London before Queen Victoria in 1887, and, after an extensive overseas tour, came home to astonishing acclaim in 1893, setting up the action in a lot located right across from the Chicago World's Fair.

The spectacle always thrilled. Cowboys— who'd once been little known, put-upon figures of cattle runs—were seen onstage as riding, roping and reliable actors in

For a time, Wild Bill Hickok (below left) reluctantly joined the cast of the play *Scout of the Plains* alongside Buffalo Bill (far right) and fellow scout/actor/cowboy "Texas Jack" Omohundro (center).

countless adventures. A little lady named Annie Oakley joined the show and shot the ashes off the cigarette in her husband's mouth, among other skills. There were Pony Express adventures, Custer's Last Stand and stagecoach robbery reenactments and finally, an Indian attack on a settler's home being defended by cowboys, led by Buffalo Bill himself. And there was no small irony that Cody hired real Native peoples to play Indian savages and supported them well through payment as actors.

Cody's thrilling extravaganzas inspired the profitable plots that would later be turned into Hollywood gold, through stars such as William S. Hart, Tom Mix, John Wayne, Randolph Scott and Clint Eastwood. As UCLA history professor Stephen Aron, PhD, puts it, "Cody, more than anyone else, monetized the wildness of the West." Adds John M. Findlay, PhD, a professor of history at the University of Washington, "Buffalo Bill was celebrating the Wild West as it was going on. I don't know how he managed to do that. He walked back and forth within reality and fiction."

Last Stand

That being the case, there is almost an inevitability to the tragedy of believing too much in one's own legend. The era of the Wild West waned in the early 1900s, and in 1903, Hollywood released *The Great Train Robbery*, the film that would both revolutionize the industry and make it much simpler for folks the world over to enjoy a Western adventure not far from home.

Cody's longtime penchant for outrageous spending and affairs had caught up with him by then, and an attempt to divorce Louisa in 1904 after years of bitter fighting was seen

as a black mark on his character. The death of his and Louisa's daughter Arta in the midst of the divorce brought untold guilt and unwanted attention. The Wild West shows had gone through several ownership changes, in no small part brought on by Cody's poor business sense, and by 1916, needing to sell his interest in the shows, he was being trundled out for appearances, a shell of his former self. His death the following year of kidney failure was the stuff of giant headlines, but creditors would eventually be required to pay for his burial. It was, in retrospect, a fall as meteoric as his rise.

"He'd always been so astoundingly physically robust and vigorous and all of those stories of him racing into the ring, there was such vitality," says Patty Limerick, PhD, faculty director and board chair of the Center of the American West at the University of Colorado Boulder. "But there seemed to be something about his frailty as an old man that was significantly escalated in melancholy because of what he had been."

After his death, Buffalo Bill became a purely fictional creature, alongside the other legends in a mythical world he essentially invented. Charlton Heston, Paul Newman, Joel McCrea, Clayton Moore, Louis Calhern, Peter Coyote and Keith Carradine were among those who wore the Cody name in film, donning the cowboy hat and riding in the kind of highly fictionalized adventures he would have enjoyed. His legend—and the one he created—lives on.

"He introduced the cowboy into the Wild West and he just had an eye for all this stuff," says White. "And even though his life in many ways ends up in disaster, he really did manage to pull off turning himself into some kind of hero." ★

FRIEND AND FOE

Buffalo Bill Cody maintained a fascinatingly unique bond with Native Americans.

It's odd to reconcile the sight of Buffalo Bill Cody standing alongside famed Sioux medicine man Sitting Bull, both looking off into the distance during the months in 1885 when the legendary Native chief took part in Buffalo Bill's Wild West. Then again, the contradiction between Cody—a man famous for his successful killings during years of Indian Wars—and the Native actors he brought into his shows is something of a head-scratcher.

The explanation comes with two justifications: commerce and respect. Given the plight of the Native people, earning good wages, even for playing roles that reinforced harmful clichés, made sense for them. The other part of the equation came with Cody recognizing the warrior aspect of the Native peoples, whom he eventually came to call "the former foe, present friend, the American."

"He recruited Lakota, with whom he got along very well, to be in the show," says Richard White, PhD, a professor emeritus of history at Stanford University. "They'd fight the whites in reality and onstage. It got so mixed up, it was just astonishing."

Perhaps it's best to see it all through the eyes of Sitting Bull, who at times was booed by audiences for being the enemy warrior. He eventually departed from the Wild West shows after finding their whole spectacle too much of a "legend" to be a part of, given that in reality, Native peoples were fighting to maintain their way of life.

"Remember, Buffalo Bill keeps it pretty tightly under control: The Lakota have only one role and that's to attack white people, and it makes it always seem as if that's what's happening," says White. "The representation they get to inhabit is a very partial one and Buffalo Bill knows what's going to sell. A performance that shows the whites dispossessing the Lakota is not going to get much of an audience."

Buffalo Bill (center) would occasionally leave his showman exploits alongside Native actors to go fight Indians.

Actor James Marsden plays sci-fi cowboy character Teddy Flood in HBO's *Westworld*

WILDER THEN— STILL WILD NOW

By 1877, Dodge City had become central to the cattle trade, with nearly 23,000 head of cattle being shipped east. That made the town a hotbed of all kinds of action.

WHERE THE ACTION WAS

DODGE CITY. TOMBSTONE. DEADWOOD.
HERE ARE THE LEGENDARY TOWNS THAT PUT
THE WILD WEST ON THE MAP—LITERALLY.

KANSAS
DODGE CITY

OPEN FOR BUSINESS
Nowadays, Dodge City is a popular tourist attraction, thanks in part to the tales Bat Masterson (below) spun.

How It Earned the Reputation

No town in the West had a worse rep than Dodge City, a haven for fast guns and faster women that even had the national media throwing shade. "Dodge City is a wicked little town," proclaimed Washington, D.C.'s newspaper *The Evening Star* back in the day. "Its character is so clearly and egregiously bad that one might conclude it was marked for special Providential punishment." The Kansas paper *Hays City Sentinel* topped that, calling Dodge a rendezvous point "for all the unemployed scalawags in seven states. Her principal business is polygamy without the sanction of religion, her code of morals is the honor of thieves." Needless to say, the town's mortality rate was staggering—but Dodge, founded in 1872, didn't have a cemetery until 1878. Until then, if you had enough money, you could be buried among the military at nearby Fort Dodge. If not, any old hole would do.

Celebrity Roll Call

Famous Dodge crime fighters included Wyatt Earp, B. W. B. "Bat" Masterson and his older brother, Ed Masterson (the latter would be killed in an 1878 gunfight), while the list of no-goodniks included Billy the Kid, Jesse James, "Dirty" Dave Rudabaugh, "Mysterious Dave" Mather and Hoodoo Brown. Mercurial gunfighter Doc Holliday —who was decent or dastardly, depending on the day—operated his dental business in Dodge for a bit, and he somehow remained on his best behavior.

How It All Began

Military outpost Fort Dodge opened on the Santa Fe Trail in 1865, primarily as a supply base but also to offer wagon trains and postal employees safe harbor from Indian attacks. Dodge City itself came about through mere happenstance: A homesteader named Henry L. Sitler built a three-room sod house on his cattle ranch, not far from the fort. Before long, hunters and traders were stopping by to set a spell. Within a year, the area's first business—a whiskey bar—opened, and soon after came a general store, a dance hall, a restaurant, a barbershop and a smithy. Originally, the settlers wanted to call this new

burg Buffalo, then found out the name had already been taken by another Kansas town. So Dodge City it was.

The Smell'll Kill Ya

Buffalo hunters and cattle rustlers—not known for hygiene—would come into Dodge, fill the Front Street establishments with the most ghastly odors imaginable and then proceed to get plastered. With 19 businesses licensed to sell booze, there was no dearth of irascible drunks. When they got too obnoxious, they were put down a 15-foot well (sometimes several men at a time) until they sobered up. Fun fact: When the train pulled up overnight in Dodge, the rail employees would visit the local brothels— the China Doll was a big favorite—taking along their red caboose lanterns in order to negotiate the dark streets. Thus the term "red-light district" was born.

This is a True Story...

...and if it ain't, it oughta be. Local folks still tell the tale of the drunken cowboy who climbed aboard the Santa Fe train in Newton, Kansas. "Where you headed?" asked the conductor. "To hell," replied the cowboy. "Well," said the conductor, "give me $2.50 and get off at Dodge, then." ★

LAW AND ORDER
Dodge City's "Peace Commission" included Bat Masterson (top photo, standing, right) and Wyatt Earp (seated, second from left), whom Masterson admired greatly.

KILLING FIELD
Along with the cattle trade, Dodge was all about the buffalo. At top, a yard with 40,000 buffalo hides.

SOUTH DAKOTA
DEADWOOD

FORTUNE SEEKERS
The old-timers (right) came and panned for gold in the Black Hills, pushing the population of the small town of Deadwood to 5,000.

ANOTHER GOLD RUSH
Col. George Armstrong Custer (below) claimed to have found gold in Deadwood and set the town on its path of infamy. It took a hotel proprietor named Seth Bullock to bring a sense of law and order to the place.

How It Earned the Reputation

It was illegal from the get-go. The settlement of Deadwood in the Black Hills of the Dakota Territory was founded in the 1870s, on sacred land that rightfully belonged to the Lakota Sioux tribe, per the 1868 Treaty of Fort Laramie. But all hell broke loose when an expedition led by Col. George Armstrong Custer claimed to have found gold. The resulting Black Hills Gold Rush brought thousands of treasure seekers to the area, out of which sprang—like a toxic weed—the infamous mining camp known as Deadwood. Whether or not Custer really

found gold is still being argued by historians, but karma had its own say years later, when the Sioux were among the tribes that slew Custer in the Battle of the Little Bighorn.

Celebrity Roll Call

Who *didn't* pop up in Deadwood? Wyatt Earp spent the winter of 1877 there, selling and delivering firewood to the settlers and leaving town with a $5,000 windfall. But big-stakes poker champ Alice Ivers easily beat that—she was winning upward of $6,000 per night, gambling in the local saloons. Years before the Sundance Kid got famous, he was jailed in Deadwood for robbing a bank. And even future POTUS Teddy Roosevelt hung out there on occasion during his stint as a deputy in Medora, North Dakota. Calamity Jane, who worked as a prostitute in several Deadwood brothels, was among the angels who treated the sick when an 1878 smallpox epidemic devastated the Black Hills. She had come to

town with sharp-shooting showman Wild Bill Hickok, who died in Deadwood upon being shot in the back while playing cards.

Law and Order

Soon after Hickok's murder, his killer, Jack McCall, was acquitted in Deadwood. But, given that Deadwood had no actual court system, a Wyoming court later agreed double jeopardy didn't apply, and he was tried again and hanged. Not long after McCall left town, a Mexican bandit was seen riding through Deadwood, boastfully displaying the severed head of an Indian, which turned out to be the last straw. Newbie resident Seth Bullock appointed himself de facto sheriff and proceeded to clean house by investigating murders, settling mining disputes and rounding up horse thieves and stagecoach robbers. He is said to have literally drawn a line across Main Street, separating the honorable people and their establishments from the deplorables. Bullock also invested $40,000 on the lavish, three-story Bullock Hotel (featuring two novelties: steam heat and indoor plumbing), which stands today. He died of cancer in 1919 in room 211, and it is said that his spirit still haunts the place.

Alternative Facts

The HBO series *Deadwood* fostered a few scenarios that simply weren't true. The real-life Al Swearengen, unlike the antihero with the marshmallow heart played by Ian McShane, was a wife-beating sex trafficker who conned women into coming to Deadwood to work at his exotic Gem Variety Theater, which featured contortionists, trapeze artists and other circus-type attractions. Once the ladies got there, he forced them into a life of prostitution. (At the time, the town had one woman to every 200 men, so there was no shortage of demand.) George Hearst, played as a gold-grubbing villain by Gerald McRaney, was actually a decent, hardworking guy of modest means. And sorry, romance fans, but Calamity Jane and Wild Bill reportedly never actually had an affair, even though they were buried side by side in Deadwood's Mount Moriah Cemetery. And what about all those F-bombs and C-words that made the HBO show sound so oddly contemporary? That's just pure hooey. "Goldarn," "dadburn" and "tarnation" was about as bad as the cussing got, back in the glory days of the real Deadwood. ★

CELEB APPEARANCES
Poker Alice Ivers (top) cleaned up the action. Theodore Roosevelt (middle) spent some time in Deadwood. Calamity Jane (below) claimed that after Wild Bill Hickok was killed, she went after his killer with a meat cleaver, having left her guns at home.

ARIZONA

TOMBSTONE

How It Earned the Reputation

They called it "The Town Too Tough to Die." Founded in 1879 by prospector Ed Schieffelin, Tombstone was a genuine boomtown—the local mines reportedly produced as much as $85 million in silver during the mid-1880s—and it boasted some 14,000 residents. Tombstone had 110 saloons, 14 gambling halls and countless brothels and—for those with more wholesome entertainment in mind—an ice cream parlor, bowling alley and opera house. It also laid claim to the legendary O.K. Corral (but more on that hokum later). What's in a name? Plenty. When Schieffelin arrived in this dangerous region—then Apache territory—he sought shelter at the U.S. Army base Fort Huachuca. According to lore, the soldiers asked Schieffelin why he so carelessly ventured out of the camp every day. "To collect rocks," Schieffelin said. Replied one of the soldiers: "You keep fooling around out there amongst them Apaches and the only rock you'll find will be your tombstone!"

Celebrity Roll Call

This here's Earp country! Virgil Earp led the local law brigade as the town marshal, backed by brothers Wyatt Earp, as deputy city marshal, and Morgan Earp, who had the title "special policeman." Always nearby, and famous in her own

STORIED FIGURES
Doc Holliday (top) spent time with girlfriend "Big Nose" Kate Horony (middle), who got a prettier retelling by Isabella Rossellini (below) in 1994's *Wyatt Earp.*

Edward Schieffelin became a millionaire, courtesy of the silver boom.

The Tombstone gunfight helped spell the end of Mattie Blaylock's time with Wyatt Earp.

right, was Mattie Blaylock, a prostitute, opium freak and loyal Earp groupie. She was Wyatt's lover—which didn't go over exceedingly well with his common-law wife, Josephine. Then there was Johnny Ringo, the renowned drunk, cattle rustler and all-around bad apple, who was among many anti-Earp sympathizers eager to put the siblings 6 feet under. He was found dead in the branches of an old oak tree, shot

The town remains part of what one historian calls a "dreamscape Southwest" that attracts many tourists.

through the head. History is hazy, and some think Wyatt did the deed. But it's just as likely that Ringo killed himself.

"Nose"-ing Around

With a girlfriend like this, who needs enemies? Doc Holliday and his Hungarian-born prostitute sweetheart "Big Nose" Kate Horony—celebrated for her prominent proboscis—came to Tombstone in 1880 and quickly became embroiled in a murder investigation. Two men had been killed in a botched stagecoach robbery in Benson, Arizona, and the county sheriff and country supervisor got "Big Nose" liquored up and convinced her to sign an affidavit stating Holliday was responsible. He was sent to the pokey, then released once his gal fessed up. No fool he, Holliday put his homely love on the next stagecoach out of Tombstone—but like a bad penny, she was back just a few months later. And since ya gotta love Hollywood, it stands to reason that "Big Nose" has been featured in several Western films, played by such world-class beauties as Faye Dunaway (1971's *Doc*), Joanna Pacula (1993's *Tombstone*) and Isabella Rossellini (1994's *Wyatt Earp*).

Spoiling for a Fight

Some historians say only 32 shots were fired in a period of 23 seconds, yet the Gunfight at the O.K. Corral looms large in the mythos of the Old West. The gist: A long feud between the Earp brothers and a group of murderous outlaws known as the Cowboys hit full boil on October 26, 1881, when the Earps and Holliday confronted five of the Cowboys and told them to surrender their weapons. This triggered a gun battle (some say Virgil fired first; others say Holliday), and when it was all over but the shouting, three of the outlaws—Tom and Frank McClaury and Billy Clanton—were dead. A fourth, Billy Claiborne, ran away, while the fifth, Ike Clanton, filed murder charges against the Earps and Holliday. (After a 30-day court hearing, all were exonerated.) Truth be told, the bloody shoot-out ought to be called the Gunfight Near the O.K. Corral, since it actually took place on Tombstone's Fremont Street, a considerable distance from the corral. ★

THE BROTHERS EARP
From top: Wyatt, Virgil and Morgan Earp reportedly tried to keep the peace in Deadwood.

REST IN PEACE
Tombstone's famous Boothill Graveyard is the resting spot for Lester Moore, a Wells Fargo station agent whose epitaph is memorable.

UTAH

THE UTAH TERRITORY

CREATING COMMUNITY
By 1877, the year Brigham Young died, more than 360 Mormon settlements were established in his "State of Deseret" (bottom).

HONEST THIEVES
Butch Cassidy (center) and the Sundance Kid (right) and their Wild Bunch did their best to keep from killing anyone on their robbing sprees.

How It Earned the Reputation

Seriously...Utah? We kid you not. Utah probably isn't the first (or even the 10th) locale you'd think of when imagining the glory days of the Old West. But its importance can't be overstated. Utah was at the very crossroads of Western traffic and had pretty much everything: pioneers, explorers, outlaws, hunters, traders, prospectors, cowboys, Indians and, most prominently, the Mormons. These members of The Church of Jesus Christ of Latter-day Saints were unwelcome in Illinois and Missouri, so they began settling in the region that is now Utah in 1847. The Mormons wanted to practice their religion in peace and isolation, and for a while, they did. But by 1849, their new home was overrun with thousands of opportunistic Easterners, passing through on their way to Gold Rush country. The Mormons petitioned the government to incorporate their land as a U.S. territory, to be called the State of Deseret. Congress didn't quite go for that, but in 1850, it officially created the Utah Territory, and President Millard Fillmore picked Brigham Young, president of the Mormon Church, to be its governor.

War Games

It didn't take long for relations to sour between the Mormons and Washington, D.C. By 1857, there was even an armed confrontation—a bit grandly known as the Utah War—that pitted the Mormon settlers against the U.S. military. It wasn't much of a skirmish, but it did fast-track the building of Camp Floyd, a government outpost in Utah's Cedar Valley that had 400 buildings and

Utah famously became the joining point of the First Transcontinental Railroad in 1869.

3,500 cavalry, infantry and artillery men—the nation's largest concentration of army troops. The Mormons also got into the fort business: With the U.S. Army fully focused on the Civil War in 1865, Brigham Young established Fort Deseret—located in western Utah—to protect his flock during the Black Hawk War. Completed in only 18 days by a team of 98 men, its 10-foot walls worked like a charm: All the locals and their livestock were hunkered down in the fort for safety when a tribal chief, Antonga—whom Young had nicknamed Black Hawk—showed up with scores of warriors, demanding that the Mormons turn over their cattle...or else. In the end, the warrior went away peacefully.

The Right Connections

The final link to the First Transcontinental Railroad—the country's first such railway—was completed in 1869 in Promontory Point, Utah, and a 17.6-karat beauty called the golden spike was driven home in the rail tracks to mark the occasion. For the centennial celebration, in 1969, a steam-powered train took 100 passengers from New York City to Promontory. Among those who hopped aboard was the greatest of all Western-movie stars, John Wayne.

Celebrity Roll Call

The saga of Butch Cassidy and the Sundance Kid is deeply rooted in Utah history. Butch (real name: Robert Leroy Parker) was the son of Mormon pioneers who settled in the area, but he got in with the wrong crowd—a miserable band of outlaws called the Wild Bunch. He later recruited Sundance (real name: Harry Alonzo Longabaugh), a bank robber from Pennsylvania, to join the club. After a wildly successful 1889 bank robbery in Telluride, Colorado (the haul was $21,000—worth $500,000 today), the gang holed up in Robber's Roost, a canyon deep in the southeastern Utah outback where Butch had stolen cattle in his youth. The Roost was so remote and well stocked with provisions that Butch and Sundance built cabins there and could relax for months at a time, free from pesky law enforcement. ★

THERE TO STAY
After Chief Antonga "Black Hawk"(top) made peace with the Mormons, other tribes continued to try to pry them away from the territory—and were all ultimately rebuffed.

MORMON LEADER
Brigham Young (above) was about 30 when he stumbled on *The Book of Mormon*; he was baptized and later became one of prophet Joseph Smith's top lieutenants.

TEXAS
FORT GRIFFIN

How It Earned the Reputation

It was hot while it lasted. Fort Griffin, a U.S. Cavalry outpost situated on the Brazos River in the north of Texas, was established in 1867 for protection from marauding Indians. It became such a popular stopover for horny cattle drivers and ruthless gunslingers that a sinful little town called Fort Griffin Flat soon mushroomed. The fort itself, which lasted a mere 14 years, was built on the cheap, due to a scarcity of materials and lack of proper funding. Yet it was so important in the fight against the Indians that, in 1871, none other than Civil War icon William Tecumseh Sherman—then commanding general of the United States Army—came by to inspect it personally. Sherman was greeted by a mob of furious settlers who claimed they were in severe danger from Indian attacks and demanded an increase in military security. Alas, he saw no such threat and decided the citizens of Fort Griffin were just a bunch of drama queens. "Toodles!" said Sherman.

Celebrity Roll Call

Wyatt Earp and Doc Holliday met and became fast friends in Fort Griffin Flat. The notorious braggart John Wesley Hardin—who claimed to have killed 42 people by the time he went to prison—was a regular in town, as was his eventual killer, the famed sheriff John Selman. Among the resident buffalo hunters was Pat Garrett, who would one day slay Billy the Kid.

Poker Face

Glamorous redhead Lottie "The Poker Queen" Deno—inspiration for the Miss Kitty character on the classic TV series *Gunsmoke*—could gamble like a man and drink like one, too. When her lover, horse jockey Johnny Golden, abandoned her and fled to the West, Lottie and her security

guard—a 7-foot-tall black nanny named Mary Poindexter—took the stagecoach to Fort Griffin. Lottie ended up a prostitute and played cards at the Bee Hive Saloon, where she was not above drawing her gun if she didn't like the way the game was going. One day, Johnny suddenly came back into her life—and, that very night, was shot dead in the alley behind the Bee Hive. Some folks don't think it's a coincidence.

Scandalous!

Fort Griffin Flat grew so rough and randy over time that it was nicknamed "Babylon on the Brazos." By 1874, the commander of the fort had enough and declared martial law. This forced many of the undesirables to head elsewhere, but that wasn't enough for the God-fearing citizens of the Flat, who successfully petitioned the Jack County Court to form their own city, naming it Albany. They also made sure Albany became the county seat, stealing the title from Fort Griffin.

And That's a Wrap

By 1881, there was little need for Fort Griffin. The buffalo herds had dwindled, which severely reduced the hunter-trader traffic. The Comanche and Kiowa tribes that once posed a threat had been put on reservations or pushed farther west, so there was no more need for military protection. But the coup de grace came when Albany raised $50,000 in bribery funds and beat out Fort Griffin to become the only local stop along the route of the new and exciting Texas Central Railroad. So on May 31, 1881, the American flag at the fort was lowered for the last time. ★

WORTH THE TRIP
The once-popular Texas town retains the flavor of its notorious past for any with a Wild West yen. The remains of Fort Griffin (above pics) are now a state of Texas historic site and tourist spot.

Rowdy roots big-time for the NFL's Cowboys, who remain one of the league's most popular teams.

OLD WEST, NEW WORLD

IN THE CURRENT DAY, THE WILD WEST HAS ONLY
EXPANDED ITS ABILITY TO CHALLENGE AND INSPIRE.

THE NFL IS ONE OF THE WORLD'S most popular sports leagues and according to *Forbes*, the Dallas Cowboys remain the most successful franchise on the planet, with a bottom line of more than $5 billion. It doesn't matter that the team hasn't won a Super Bowl since 1996 (except to Cowboys fans); its followers, spurred on by the 20-gallon-hat-wearing, water-pistol-shooting mascot Rowdy, keep accruing T-shirts and caps and buying into the brand's view of the Cowboys as "America's Team."

But what of Dallas' big division rivals, Washington? The championship drought is even longer for them, with 1992 being the last time they raised the Vince Lombardi Trophy. And while both Dallas and Washington each have wealthy team owners who sometimes sow the seeds of dissatisfaction, for Washington, the biggest controversy of more recent years has involved the team's name.

In today's lens, the name "Redskins" is seen as a slur by many on the proud legacy of Native Americans. The debate, a part of the national conversation since the 1990s, has gained strength since 2013. In 2020, pressure from the NFL and corporate sponsors had team owner Daniel Snyder, who had long stood by the name, finally change his tune—and the team's moniker. Plenty of other sports teams have also heard the call and made a change that deflects the "legacy of negativity" some groups say the word redskin perpetuates. In 1995, for instance, St. John's University in NYC altered its sports teams' names from the Redmen to the Red Storm.

Decades ago, this controversy would not have been on too many folks' radar, and that says a great deal about how the Wild West spirit—still celebrated from sea to shining sea in the United States—has evolved in America. While the phrase still suggests pride and individualism in everything from the internet to print media, history has skewed the meaning Hollywood long gave to the period. The more people accept the truth of what happened during those notorious days, the deeper the meaning becomes. And more folks and groups have been able to take ownership of their tales as well, in literature, the movies, television and in a world at large that's seen the word "coronavirus" enter the vernacular with a vengeance.

"Beyond all the layers of fiction, that phrase becomes central to who Americans think they are," says John M. Findlay, PhD, a professor of history at the University of Washington. "The American people have constantly put themselves out in the wilderness, or up against savagery, and that experience shapes us. And we're always having to reinvent our institutions—like reinventing democracy. And 'reinventing' is what makes us who we are."

The Myths About the Myths

The definition used to be so much more black and white. Starting in the mid-20th century, the Wild West myth was as American as baseball, apple pie and a pack of cigarettes in your shirt pocket. The heroes we looked up to in the movies and on TV wore Stetsons and tin stars, with John Wayne ruling at the box office.

LARGER THAN LIFE
Wild Bill Hickok was shot dead in Deadwood; the man remains a local attraction (above left) and the old town itself inspired a quality TV drama on HBO (center).

PAYING RESPECTS
"End of the Trail," at the National Cowboy & Western Heritage Museum (top), captures the courageous history of Native plight.

Even when things grew more complicated starting in the anti-hero days of the 1960s, the characters wreaking havoc with sawed-off shotguns or a pair of Peacemakers were still worth looking up to for maintaining a sense of justice. And in many cases, top politicians took a page out of Teddy Roosevelt's political playbook to get to the White House. Granted, George H. W. Bush had been a Houston oilman and George W. Bush the governor of Texas, so the wide-brim hats they sometimes wore made sense. And while Ronald Reagan had only been governor of California, he'd also played Gen. Custer in the 1940 film *Santa Fe Trail*. More than a century after its most famous names lived big (and decades since the days when Hollywood helped carve those names into the American consciousness), the Wild West still stands as a time and place where the seemingly endless spaces became like one big challenge. The charter was to explore, to win, to expand and to leave your mark in as loud and significant a way as possible. Even today, the ghosts of that era—including political leaders—still inspire people to dream big and press forward without fail.

But in the past few decades, the Wild West's notoriety has seen a shift, with greater attention paid to life beyond the stalwart myths it always represented. While the words still refer to anything that remains wild and untamed—from the 2016 Oregon cattle rancher standoff, to the roller-coaster route of the 2020 financial markets in the wake of the COVID-19 crisis, to Facebook privacy rules—they've also been used to update the American narrative.

That may be best seen in the movies and on TV. The 2016 film *Hell or High Water* updates the Western to now include a pair of notorious current-day brothers who rob banks in order to save their West Texas ranch from foreclosure. The HBO series and movie *Deadwood* brought much more modern language, themes and storytelling to the tale of the South Dakota town that set the template for violence in the Old West (although chances are, things weren't quite as violent as the series suggests). And most notably, *Westworld* (also on HBO) constructs, unravels and then completely rebuilds the myths, in a show about a realistic, robotic Western amusement park. As the seasons go on, the show comes to take a deeper look into how the high-stakes world of technology has become the real Wild West of the modern day. The question the show asks is: Who really controls the narrative? And that, more than anything, seems to represent the new Wild West idea. Or, as Stanford University history professor emeritus Richard White, PhD, puts it, "That whole story of the American belief that your fate is in your hands finds its manifestation in the West."

Riding Off Into the Sunset

And yet, there's no tossing away the more comfortable, and comforting, ideas of the West. We know how hard the life of the cowboy was on the cattle trail, even the irony that the very symbol of independence turned out to be an underpaid wageworker badly in need of a raise or a good union. And there's no denying that this iconic figure has been somewhat in decline; the last Clint Eastwood Western was the Oscar-winning *Unforgiven*, which came out when the Redskins won their last NFL title nearly 30 years ago.

Still, in many circles, we embrace and revere what the cowboy has long stood for. "There are certain places in our country, like Texas and Oklahoma, and Kansas to a certain extent, and Wyoming, where they seize on their participation in the open-range cattle industry as a way for them to have a special claim on cowboys," suggests Findlay. That doesn't keep it from being a little more complicated. Oklahoma City is the center for the National Cowboy & Western Heritage Museum and, says Findlay, "in that way, they can keep the cowboys and Indians, and rodeos and all that stuff alive and feed off it as a way for them to participate in this Western identity." But some adjustments are necessary. "It's no longer politically correct to have a lot of Western art that denigrates Native Americans, so the museums have found ways to welcome Native American participation. And in fact, the Gilchrist Museum in Tulsa was founded by an oilman who was part Native American. There is this kind of mixture in these displays that can't help but be controversial if it glorified conquests of Native peoples."

Perhaps the saving grace comes in accepting the same decline in the traditional idea of cowboys and Indians that has led to the change in sports team names. The Wild West view can't help but be affected by the truths that have emerged in the decades since.

That won't ever truly change the mythical West's power to inspire any individual with the dream of making a name for him—or her—self. It will only continue to grow the definition's breadth. It's what Patty Limerick, PhD, faculty director and board chair of the Center of the American West at the University of Colorado Boulder, seems to suggest when talking about *The Virginian*, Owen Wister's 1902 novel that set Hollywood on its decades-long quest to celebrate the era. "The book seems to be a statement about the Wild West," she says, "but it's also such a strange, convoluted statement about what it means to be tough." ★

TAKING A RIDE
The stagecoach still goes up the main thoroughfare in Tombstone, Arizona, but it's there to bring back mythic memories, not deliver gunslingers to the O.K. Corral.

COVER (Background) Reinhold Leitner/Shutterstock (Flag) Leigh Prather/Shutterstock (Clockwise from top left) Chronicle/ Alamy Stock Photo; Ian Dagnall/Alamy Stock Photo; GL Archive/Alamy Stock Photo; mikeledray/Shutterstock; WikiMedia Commons; GL Archive/Alamy Stock Photo; Bettmann/Getty Images; adoc-photos/Getty Images; jvphoto/Alamy Stock Photo **FRONT FLAP** John Swartz Archive/Getty Images **2-3** YinYang/Getty Images **4** (Clockwise from top left) Universal History Archive/Getty Images; GraphicaArtis/Getty Images; Everett Collection; Ed Vebell/Getty Images **6-7** danm/ Getty Images **8** Hulton Deutsch/Getty Images **10** (Clockwise from top) Shawshots/Alamy Stock Photo; Pictorial Press Ltd/ Alamy Stock Photo; WikiMedia Commons **11** (Clockwise from top left) mauritius images GmbH/Alamy Stock Photo; GL Archive/Alamy Stock Photo; Everett Historical/Shutterstock; Bettmann/Getty Images; GL Archive/Alamy Stock Photo; Universal History Archive/Universal Images Group via Getty Images; Basement Stock/Alamy Stock Photo **12** outdoorsman/ Shutterstock **14** W. Scott McGill/Shutterstock **15** Popperfoto/Getty Images **16** North Wind Picture Archives/Alamy Stock Photo **17** (From left) PF-(bygone1)/Alamy Stock Photo; North Wind Picture Archives/Alamy Stock Photo **18** MPI/Getty Images **20-21** (Clockwise from top left) Otto Herschan Collection/Getty Images; Everett Collection Historical/Alamy Stock Photo; Hulton Archive/Getty Images **22** MPI/Getty Images **23** (From top) Universal History Archive/Getty Images; WikiMedia Commons **24** Underwood Archives/UIG/Shutterstock **27** (From left) PhotoQuest/Getty Images; MPI/Getty Images **28** Buyenlarge/Getty Images **29** UniversalImagesGroup/Getty Images **30** MPI/Getty Images **32** Bettmann/Getty Images **34** Courtesy of the Library of Congress **35** (From top) Print Collector/Getty Images; Courtesy of the Library of Congress **36** (From top) Universal History Archive/Getty Images; Courtesy of the Library of Congress **37** (From top) History and Art Collection/Alamy Stock Photo; GL Archive/Alamy Stock Photo; AF archive/Alamy Stock Photo **38** (Clockwise from top left) American Stock Archive/Getty Images; Bettmann/Getty Images; MPI/Getty Images **39** (Clockwise from top) John van Hasselt - Corbis/Sygma via Getty Images; Pictorial Parade/Getty Images; John van Hasselt - Corbis/Sygma via Getty Images **40** (From top) Anonymous/AP/Shutterstock; GL Archive/Alamy Stock Photo; Courtesy of the Library of Congress **41** (From top) Courtesy of the Library of Congress; Courtesy of the Detroit Free Press; Fotosearch/Getty Images **42** (From top) Courtesy Everett Collection; Bettmann/Getty Images **43** (From top) John Swartz Archive/Getty Images; AF archive/ Alamy Stock Photo **44** FLHC25/Alamy Stock Photo **45** WikiMedia Commons **46** Universal History Archive/Getty Images **48** (From top) Everett Historical/Shutterstock; Pictorial Press Ltd/Alamy Stock Photo **49** (From top) WikiMedia Commons; FLHC14/Alamy Stock Photo **50** (From top) WikiMedia Commons (2); Courtesy of the Library of Congress **51** (From top) WikiMedia Commons; GL Archive/Alamy Stock Photo **52** (From left) Jonathan Blair/Getty Images; Universal History Archive/Universal Images Group via Getty Images **54** Bettmann/Getty Images (2) **55** (From left) Everett Collection Inc/ Alamy Stock Photo; Bettmann/Getty Images **56** (From left) Hulton Archive/Getty Images; WikiMedia Commons; ullstein bild/Getty Images **57** Smith Collection/Gado/Getty Images **58** (From left) Hulton Archive/Getty Images; Bettmann/ Getty Images **59** (From left) Fototeca Storica Nazionale./Getty Images; UtCon Collection/Alamy Stock Photo; WikiMedia Commons; TopFoto/Alamy Stock Photo **60** Courtesy Everett Collection **62** General Photographic Agency/Getty Images **63-72** Courtesy Everett Collection (8) **73** ©Touchstone Pictures/Courtesy Everett Collection **74** duncan1890/Getty Images **76** Greg Kuchik/Getty Images **78** (Clockwise from top left) WikiMedia Commons; Courtesy of the Library of Congress; n_defender/Shutterstock; Courtesy of the Library of Congress **79** (From top) Billion Photos/Shutterstock; C Squared Studios/ Getty Images **80** (Clockwise from top) Alan Majchrowicz/Alamy Stock Photo; Paul R. Jones/Shutterstock; Courtesy of the Library of Congress **81** David J. Green/Alamy Stock Photo **82** Olivier Le Queinec/Shutterstock **84** (Clockwise from top) Vintage Images/Alamy Stock Photo; GL Archive/Alamy Stock Photo; Delpixel/Shutterstock **85** Courtesy of the Library of Congress **86** (From top) North Wind Picture Archives/Alamy Stock Photo; bjsites/Shutterstock; Shelly Still/Shutterstock; Creative Studio/Shutterstock **87** (From top) INTERFOTO/Alamy Stock Photo; LI Cook/Shutterstock; Daniel Ladd/Alamy Stock Photo **88** Mark Lisk/Alamy Stock Photo **89** (From top) Pete Hoffman/Shutterstock; MPI/Getty Images **90** Science History Images/Alamy Stock Photo **92** Rick Pisio/RWP Photography/Alamy Stock Photo **93** (From top) Science History

Images/Alamy Stock Photo; Basement Stock/Alamy Stock Photo **94-95** (Clockwise from top) Library of Congress/Corbis/ VCG via Getty Images; Collection Christophel/Alamy Stock Photo; ©20thCentFox/Courtesy Everett Collection; MPI/Getty Images (2); Historic Images/Alamy Stock Photo; Bettmann/Getty Images **96** Ed Vebell/Getty Images **98-99** Buyenlarge/ Getty Images **100** (From top) JRLPhotographer/Getty Images; Sepia Times/Getty Images **101** Courtesy Everett Collection **102** PhotoQuest/Getty Images **104** AF archive/Alamy Stock Photo **105** (Clockwise from top left) WikiMedia Commons; Roberto Trivella/EyeEm/Getty Images; Elwood Hofer/Getty Images **106** Herbert/Stringer/Getty Images **107** (From top) WikiMedia Commons; Ivy Close Images/Alamy Stock Photo **108** MPI/Getty Images **111** Bettmann/Getty Images **112** (From left) WikiMedia Commons; Vintage Images/Alamy Stock Photo **114** Bettmann/Getty Images **116** David Madison/Getty Images **118** North Wind Picture Archives/Alamy Stock Photo **119** Georgia Evans/Shutterstock **120** T photography/ Shutterstock **121** (From top) Lydmila Grekul/Shutterstock; WikiMedia Commons (2) **122** Rosanne Tackaberry/Alamy Stock Photo **124** Stock Montage/Getty Images 125 Buyenlarge/Getty Images 126 GraphicaArtis/Getty Images **127** DEA/G. DAGLI ORTI/Getty Images **128** steve bly/Alamy Stock Photo **129-130** Courtesy of the Library of Congress (2) **131** ROBYN BECK/ Getty Images **132** Buyenlarge/Getty Images **134** (Clockwise from top left) ullstein bild Dtl./Getty Images; INTERFOTO/ Alamy Stock Photo; SN VFX/Shutterstock; INTERFOTO/Alamy Stock Photo **135** (From top) PictureLux/The Hollywood Archive/Alamy Stock Photo; INTERFOTO/Alamy Stock Photo **136** (From left) WikiMedia Commons; INTERFOTO/Alamy Stock Photo (2) **137** (From top) LMPC/Getty Images; INTERFOTO/Alamy Stock Photo **138** Print Collector/Getty Images **140** Library of Congress/Getty Images **142** Smith Collection/Gado/Getty Images **143** Bettmann/Getty Images **144** Hulton Archive/Getty Images **146** Universal History Archive/UIG/Shutterstock **148** American Stock Archive/Getty Images **150** Stock Montage/Getty Images **151** ©United Artists/Courtesy Everett Collection **152-154** WikiMedia Commons (2) **155** Courtesy of True West magazine **156** WikiMedia Commons (3) **157** (From top) Courtesy Everett Collection; ©20thCentFox/Courtesy Everett Collection (2) **158** American Stock Archive/Getty Images **160** Buyenlarge/Getty Images **161** Bettmann/Getty Images **163** Collection Christophel/Alamy Stock Photo **165** Bettmann/Getty Images **166** Bad Robot/Kobal/Shutterstock **168** Fotosearch/Getty Images **170** (From top) Danita Delimont/Alamy Stock Photo; WikiMedia Commons **171** (From left) Science History Images/Alamy Stock Photo; World Archive/Alamy Stock Photo **172** (From top) North Wind Picture Archives/Alamy Stock Photo; Carol M. Highsmith/WikiMedia Commons; APIC/Getty Images **173** (Clockwise from top left) Glasshouse Images/Alamy Stock Photo; WikiMedia Commons; Hulton Archive/Getty Images; GraphicaArtis/Getty Images **174** (Clockwise from top left) Pictorial Press Ltd/Alamy Stock Photo; WikiMedia Commons (2); ©Warner Bros/ Courtesy Everett Collection; WikiMedia Commons **175** (Clockwise from top left) Lou GRIVE/Gamma-Rapho via Getty Images; Pictorial Parade/Getty Images; WikiMedia Commons; FLHC 1C/Alamy Stock Photo; Franck Fotos/Alamy Stock Photo **176** (From left) Universal History Archive/UIG via Getty Images; World History Archive/Alamy Stock Photo; Science History Images/Alamy Stock Photo **177** (Clockwise from top left) GraphicaArtis/Getty Images; Patrick Guenette/Alamy Stock Vector; Universal History Archive/UIG via Getty Images **178** (From left) Archive Pics/Alamy Stock Photo; Pictorial Press Ltd/Alamy Stock Photo; WikiMedia Commons **179** (From left) Alpha Stock/Alamy Stock Photo; Prisma by Dukas Presseagentur GmbH/Alamy Stock Photo **180** (From top) Wesley Hitt/Getty Images; Matthew Pearce/Icon Sportswire via Getty Images **182-183** (From left) Chicago Tribune/Getty Images; ©HBO/Courtesy Everett Collection; Peter Bischoff/Getty Images **184** imageBROKER/Shutterstock **185** Ken Howard/Alamy Stock Photo **SPINE** wwing/Getty Images **BACK FLAP** Ed Vebell/Getty Images **BACK COVER** (From top) Buyenlarge/Getty Images; WikiMedia Commons; Buyenlarge/Getty Images

Special thanks to contributing writer Michael Logan

CENTENNIAL BOOKS

An Imprint of
Centennial Media, LLC
40 Worth St., 10th Floor
New York, NY 10013, U.S.A.

ISBN 978-1-951274-35-1

Distributed by
Simon & Schuster, Inc.
1230 Avenue of the Americas
New York, NY 10020, U.S.A.

For information about custom editions, special sales and premium and corporate purchases,
please contact Centennial Media at contact@centennialmedia.com.

Manufactured in China

10 9 8 7 6 5 4 3 2 1

Publishers & Co-Founders Ben Harris, Sebastian Raatz
Editorial Director Annabel Vered
Creative Director Jessica Power
Executive Editor Janet Giovanelli
Deputy Editors Ron Kelly, Alyssa Shaffer
Design Director Martin Elfers
Art Directors Patrick Crowley,
Natali Suasnavas, Joseph Ulatowski
Copy / Production Patty Carroll, Angela Taormina
Assistant Art Director Jaclyn Loney
Photo Editor Kim Kuhn
Production Manager Paul Rodina
Production Assistant Alyssa Swiderski
Editorial Assistant Tiana Schippa
Sales & Marketing Jeremy Nurnberg